ISBN 978-1-7367625-1-6
Moon over the Mountain Press

A Broom at Midnight:
13 Gates of Witchcraft
by Spirit Flight

Roger J. Horne

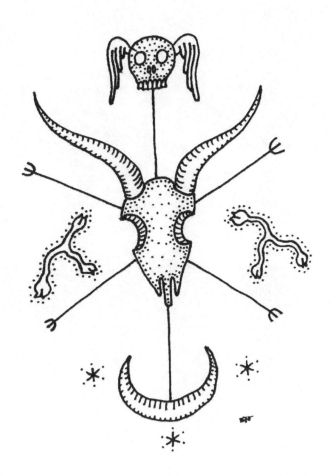

In Benevento a nut-tree stands,
And thither by night from many lands,
Over the waters and on the wind,
Come witches flying of every kind,
On goats, and boars, and bears, and cats,
Some upon broomsticks, some like bats,
Howling, hurtling, hurrying, all,
Come to the tree at the master's call.

-Charles G. Leland (1892) translating Dom Piccini's
Ottava della Notte

Contents

Foreword

This book and its author are indebted to the masters of craft who have come before, to my ancestors, those Scottish highland charmers and mountain herb-doctors, to the many folklorists who have heard and preserved the lore for future generations, and to my own familiars who have and continue to teach me along the path.

The book you now hold, reader, is divided into an introductory segment and thirteen main chapters, followed by a ritual appendix. These thirteen methods and folkloric threads of transvective witchery offer mere pieces of a greater whole. By exploring these thirteen approaches in spirit flight, it is my hope that the student witch will experiment, adapt, and perhaps explore their own ancestral and regional practices, developing their own individual repertoire of craft. The charms and lore of each chapter are grounded thoroughly in sourced knowledge so that those texts may be accessed for further learning, but much of our craft is ingrained in stories and in oral tradition, which makes this manner of work difficult. I have nonetheless tried my best to provide further texts for the benefit of young and budding witches growing into their own craft.

The appendix at the end of this book contains truncated outlines of the rites described in each chapter for the practitioner's easy reference.

The charms represented in this work call upon the Devil unapologetically and allude to saints and adaptations of the Latin language of the church. The presence of "sains" and "paternosters" will not bother those of us familiar with folk craft, particularly Scottish witchery, but for those coming to these words from a New Age perspective, it is wise to remember that the ancestors of modern folk witch traditions are those cunning crafters, wise women, charmers, and fairy doctors of old who adapted and appropriated Christian liturgy for their own purposes, both benevolent and malevolent. These liturgical threads are authentic, and though they are not present in all of the charms here, the idea of washing them away entirely pains me.

Similarly, some may be uncomfortable with the degree to which this book calls on the Devil, the Man in Black, and even explores the symbolism of Lucifer himself. There is no white-washing, no erasing, no tiptoeing around the plain fact that those charmers of old who have bequeathed their craft to us called upon dark and dreadful entities from the abyss. These operations are recorded both in lore and in the multitude of grimoires circulating in the medieval and early modern periods. It is important, however, to note that the Devil of many folk charms is not quite the same as the Devil of modern Christianity; they are in many facets divergent figures. One an ancestor, Old One, trickster, and master of hidden art, emblematic of the first practitioners of our craft, and the other a two-dimensional character who is merely a distorted mirror image of the Christian deity.

A repeated motif in this exploration of transvective craft is the image I call the glyph or sigil of the crossroads, the intersection of its three lines representing at once the central festivals of All Hallows' Eve, Yule, Candlemas, May Eve, Midsummer, and Lammas, but also representing the crossroads and the convergence of consciousness at work in the achievement of sabbatic ekstasis, a state devoid of time or space entirely. This simple formation of three lines intersecting is, in simpler historical terms, the asteriskos of the ancient world, the root of today's asterisk. D'Arcy (2017) notes that this symbol is among the most ancient paintings found in ice age caves occupied by early humans, its simple lines suggesting a star, a light, or a convergence of paths. Its beams are evocative of the brightness of Venus, the morning star.

Lastly, I would like to note that this book came to fruition in the wake of a pandemic that has throttled the world. As a person with immunocompromised loved ones who live in near-constant fear of this virus, I have had my share of worry, but in truth, I have been fortunate. Many have experienced loneliness and isolation in these times, and many have lost loved ones who should be with us today. The suffering in this world is great right now, but I am comforted by the threads that bind and unite the practitioners of our art, even through walls (both real and metaphorical) and invisibly across miles of land and sea. Even between you and I, reader, there is a communion of *spirits as you read these words. I am grateful to you, and I wish for you those precious blessings of health, happiness, and safe togetherness with your kin—in this world and the other.*

The Transvective Arts in Context

Through keyholes and twisted trees, by moonlight and candlelight, across oceans and fields and forests, witches fly. This is something even children know. It is ingrained in the lore of cultures around the world. What is less understood in modern times is the inherent symbolism of witch-flight, which together forms a body of lore-born wisdom. The actual praxis of engaging in flight—the charms, rituals, and recipes associated with this tradition of our art—is even less understood.

Part of the problem lies in the diverse means and forms of folk witchcraft as a whole and our inability to make sense of its symbolism, abstraction, and pluralism when every other area of learning in our lives is governed by the cold science of empiricism. The other part of the challenge to understanding traditions of spirit flight is the romanticization of witchcraft that took place in popular literature from the early 1900s to sometime in the 1990s, exaggerating the role of the "hidden cult" and hiding the reality of folk craft practices in plain sight.

Nonetheless, witches are at this moment coming home to their ancestral, lore and land-based folk traditions in droves never before seen. Disillusioned with the New Age movement and the attempt to forge a "one-size-fits-all" model of craft, witches are again exploring the old lore and charms of our ancestors, wresting them from obscurity and reinvigorating them with modern approach. The old grimoires and folkloric texts are again popular, and our ancestors smile on us as we experiment and develop our methodology to working charms that were once old, but are now new again.

Among these, the rediscovered practice of transvection or spirit flight has enjoyed special popularity. Perhaps it is our desire for freedom. Perhaps it is our need of the more direct forms of instruction and initiation in witchcraft provided by the powers of the otherworld. Whatever the reason, the old lore and charms of spirit flight are coming unearthed, much to the pleasure of folk and traditional witches who have preserved these arts. The tenth century *Canon Episcopi* describes popular beliefs around the witch's art of flight in fantastical detail, though as we shall see, the images here contain at least a seed of truth:

> Seduced by the fantastic illusion of demons, [witches] insist that they ride at night on certain beasts alongside the pagan goddess, Diana, and many other women; they cross vast distances in the silence of deepest night; they obey the wills of the goddess as if she were their mistress; on particular nights they are called to wait on her.

Even the meaning of the word *hagazussa*, a common term for practitioners of our art in Old High German, refers both to *witch* and *hag of the fence*, suggesting a connection between the witch and the ability to cross boundaries between civilization and the wilderness—or the known world and the unseen world of mystery. Modern witches operating within Germanic and Saxon traditional currents sometimes refer to themselves as "hedge witches" or "hedge-riders" for this reason, the hedge representing a symbolic boundary between worlds.

Spirit flight, at its most basic level, refers to the very real and practical methods of transvection practiced mainly by folk and traditional witches around the world in order to depart from the physical body and attend to various spiritual affairs. These practices are diverse and nuanced. Some involve elaborate rituals, while others (often my personal favorites) are incredibly simple and to-the-point. Some rely on the preparation of particular oils and unguents that have, in recent years, been referred to as a part of veneficium or the "poison path." Others rely on skills that can be developed using what is available to the witch in his or her own environment, making do with what is local and what is on hand.

The transvective arts employed by our ancestors in magical flight are at least as old as animism itself, the natural spirituality of indigenous cultures around the world. Animism is a loose term used to describe a diverse breadth of spiritual practices that were once considered "primitive" by archaeologists, usually involving a recognition of a diverse world of spirits mirroring and evident in the natural world of flora and fauna. The practice of animism also recognizes the reality of magic and the otherworld. We see in the cave paintings of our ancient ancestors depictions of the human spirit leaving the body to journey to other worlds, sometimes shapeshifting into other animal or spirit forms. Jakobsen's (1999) scholarship on the history of shamanism offers a helpful perspective on what he calls "magical flight," in that these figures, appearing in Neolithic paintings around the world, seem to depict not only a skilled magical practitioner, but a mediator between worlds who traveled to and from the otherworld in order to procure remedies and forge helpful relationships with the spirits that governed nature. Risley (1901), whose writings are flawed and tainted with the prevalent racism of their time, nonetheless illuminates the key point that animism, in contrast to modern religion, does not shy away from the dark aspects inherent in the natural world:

> What the Animist worships and seeks by all means to influence and conciliate is the shifting and shadowy company of unknown powers or influences...in the primeval forest, in the crumbling hills, in the rushing river, in the spreading tree; which gives its spring to the tiger, its venom to the snake...

We modern witches shall forgive the archaeologists and folklorists their inability to recognize the surviving animism in our modern traditions. While scholars are helpful in their capacity to examine and illuminate connections across cultures, they do not help us achieve the flight we seek. Rather, they give us the vocabulary to begin to understand how ancient and central to the human experience spirit flight really is. Given this perspective, it is not strange that witches fly, but rather, strange to think that we are among the few who still do, our folk traditions preserving a body of practices so ancient and natural to the human spirit that they elude modern religion altogether and become the basis of strange tales told on winter nights.

Much of the mystery surrounding the flight practices of witches is shrouded in a central question of agency and inherent or learned ability. Although writers in the medieval and early modern eras acknowledged that witches flew in spirit and not necessarily in body, they did not always agree on praxis, the specific charms noted ranging from salve to staff to weed. Isobel Gowdie, a famous Scottish witch, described the experience of being swept away to the otherworld frequently, seemingly against her will (Wilby, 2010). In older accounts, it is unclear sometimes whether the minds of the time believed witches to be inherently gifted with flight or individuals who employed specific, learned spiritual practices. If we modern practitioners acknowledge dream and ecstasy as inherently magical acts (which we should), then we must in some ways accept that there is at least a predisposition to spirit flight in certain people. These things come more easily to some than to others. At the same time, it serves us well to approach spirit flight as a magical discipline with specific operations, charms, and practices that can aid us in perfecting our art.

The famous Abramelin text, derived from magical manuscripts written in either the early 1600s or 1400s, describes a witch employing a salve that causes the experience of flight. This and similar accounts have motivated a great deal of research into the roles of psychoactive ointments, oils, and other preparations relying on alkaloids present in the famous witches' nightshades, usually henbane, datura, belladonna, or mandrake. The psychoactive properties of this family of plants, though very real, have been somewhat exaggerated in terms of any safe, practical dosage for modern use; the dosage required to achieve a delirious state is dangerously close to a lethal dose. Still, the use of specific nightshade preparations at a very low and precise dosage would (and for many modern witches, still does) achieve a slight level of inebriation conducive to trance (Ratsch, 2005).

Similarly, many texts have noted the use of the staff or broom as an aid to flight. The proceedings against Alice Kyteler in 1324 note that she anointed a staff, thereby imbuing it with the power of flight (Wright, 1843). Hatsis (2015) notes that this isn't merely derivative of the properties of the ointment transferred to the skin; many sources note that the witch's staff or broom, sometimes given as a gift from the devil, does itself possess the necessary magic to aid in flight. Scot (1584) put forward that witches rode "invisiblie through the aire" via dreaming, while their bodies lay soundly asleep in their beds. We'll return to all of these subjects in greater detail when we explore each gate to spirit flight individually.

The corpus of charm and ritual we will be exploring in this volume clearly holds at least a superficial similarity to other modern practices, such as shamanic journeying and pathworking. Unlike these sister traditions, however, the folk witch's art of transvection does not include scripted encounters with a learned cosmology. Its experience is not predictable in the manner of a memory palace. Rather, the witch's practice of spirit flight, though conducted via specific charms and rituals, is more spontaneous in nature—a calling from the deep and dark that is heard and answered in the language of ritual. Its goals are more diverse and nuanced as well. While spirit flight can be used to derive new charms, sigils, and knowledge from the denizens of the otherworld, sometimes called Elphame, it can also facilitate a kind of communion of otherly souls that has been called the witches' sabbat. In drinking from this well, witches experience a kind of nourishment of the soul. Flight can also be conducted for less lofty purposes: to perform craft upon an intended target who is many miles away (sometimes referred to as sending "the hag" or "the fetch"), to divine wisdom from spirits, to contact the dead, to form new relationships with potential familiar spirits, and many other reasons that will be described in more detail in the chapters of this book, for this systematic exploration of methodology is the precise aim of this work. In the process, we will see that the witch's craft of transvection is not a singular, paradigmatic practice, but a diverse body of ecstatic arts, rich in tradition and nuance, and all worthy of exploration. *Spirit flight*, then, is not merely one art, but an umbrella term for a body of practices bound up in a single concept. Each of these gates offers something new and wondrous in its own terms, and though the practitioner will naturally develop an inclination towards a particular tradition of transvection, it serves the student witch well to explore many.

Riding with Devils

The otherworld is unlike our own. Its forms and phenomena have been described as nightmarish when experienced by non-witches. When Michael Schenck famously experimented with the internal use of henbane, a well-known witches' herb, he described horrifying visions:

> ...there were terrifying stones and clouds of mist, all sweeping along in the same direction. They called me irresistibly with them. Their coloring must be described—but it was not a pure hue. They enveloped a vague gray light, which emitted a dull glow and rolled onward and upward into a black and smoky sky. I was flung into a flaring drunkenness, a witches' cauldron of madness. Above my head, water was flowing, dark and blood-red. The sky was filled with herds of animals. Fluid, formless creatures emerged from the darkness. I heard words, but they were all wrong and nonsensical, and yet they possessed for me some hidden meaning. (Kulkin, 1999)

Schenck's account is even more harrowing due to

the experimental use of a known deliriant nightshade in a concentration and dosage far beyond any that a modern witch would use, but his description echoes the tales of those who wander into the otherworld without adequate knowledge and preparation. Robert Kirk's (1691) description of otherworldly denizens includes a tale of a woman kidnapped by spirits, then later returned to her home. She describes her experience during her two years of imprisonment thusly:

> ...she perceived little what they did in the spacious house she lodged in until she anointed one of her eyes with a certain unction that was by her; which they perceiving to have acquainted her with their actions, they made her blind of that eye with a puff of their breath. She found the place full of light, without any fountain or lamp from whence it did spring.

Another similar account provided by Kirk describes a kidnapped person who "saw and conversed with a people she knew not, having wandered in seeking of her sheep and slept upon a hill, finding herself transported to another place..." These tales echo the patterns of well-known folklore and fairy tales, from the girl in "Mother Holle," who finds another world down a well, to the child in the "The Three Spinners," who encounters an otherworldly trinity of beings with seemingly strange goals and purposes.

For the folk witch, however, encounters with the otherworld are a crucial source of knowledge, growth, and spiritual nourishment. There is something in the heart of the witch that craves ecstatic escape into the wild and dark. Whether through the use of alcohol, herbs, ritual, or charms, witches are possessed of a seeking nature that sends us tunneling into the hidden realm, and perhaps it is due to this innate yearning that we are able to see spirits of the otherworld as kindred beings.

Much like the natural world, with its diverse ecosystems and interdependent kingdoms of flora and fauna, the spiritual world is neither good nor evil. There are predators and prey. Some relationships between beings are mutually beneficial, while others are parasitic and harmful. For the witch, a voyage into the otherworld via spirit flight is undertaken with the same attitude as a walk in the woods: full of wonder and respect— but also care. The beings of the otherworld are not all friendly or safe, nor are they evil demons intent on tormenting us. A snake is not evil because it eats a bird; a bird is not good because it sings a pretty song. If we are to approach the spiritual beings of the otherworld with the care and respect they deserve, we must shed this old skin and learn to look at other autonomous beings without preconception.

While the language of ecology is roomy

and complex, the fractured language of Christianity, with its divine angels and infernal devils, is an ill fit. Perhaps this is why witch-lore from the early modern period is so ambiguous about the cosmological relationship between Elphame—the realm of elves, faeries, and witches—and Hell. While church figures considered them one and the same, the testimonies of those who described experiences in Elphame were clear and insistent that it was a separate place, though similarly subterranean and located in some proximity to Hell itself (Howard, 2013). The incongruity between the old folk beliefs of paganism and the new religion created strange cosmologies indeed.

Despite the demonization of faeries, elves, and ancestral and land-based spirits, witches have and continue to seek relationships with the spirit world. The villainization the church used to paint a frightening picture of these beings is not unlike the villainization of the figure of the witch herself; in fact, we often find in the lore that witches are treated as the descendants or distant relatives of those regarded as faeries or fallen angels. In *Aradia*, Leland (1899) describes the mythological first witch as a descendant of a fallen angel named Lucifer and the moon goddess, Diana, and places faeries firmly under the rulership of Diana, who is also the "queen of witches all." Similarly, the Book of Enoch, an ancient Hebrew text dated around

300 B.C.E., describes the fallen angels who came to earth to teach human beings their hidden arts and to couple with them, creating a hybrid race different from the line of Adam and Eve. Our witch-lore may not offer us a literal history, but it offers a way of understanding a key truth that guides our work with spirits: for witches, the beings of the otherworld are not our enemies, our subordinates, our servants, or our masters. They are our kin.

In fact, the principle of kinship is so essential to my approach to spirit work that I would not, under any circumstance, enter into an arrangement with a spirit I could not *feel* was my kin. It is something one feels deeply and unmistakably, a jarring and inexplicable sense of connection and communion, like recognizing a parent or grandparent after being apart for too long. Under certain circumstances, even those spirits that have been maligned and described as infernal, wrathful creatures in medieval grimoires can surprise us. Imagine the surprise of the witch who conjures a well-catalogued goetic demon and finds that the creature within the scrying mirror is not so unlike himself. Much like the witch, these spirits have been demonized for thousands of years and catalogued under so many names that their original deific roles have been all but erased by time, their temples buried, their worship stamped out by the brutality of new religions.

In building respectful, nourishing relationships with spirits, even dark spirits, the witch liberates those maligned and ostracized parts of herself. A hopeful witch might begin acquiring a familiar by making small offerings and utilizing divination to better understand the nature, sigil, and name of a spirit that has appeared to them. These practices will be explored more in the chapters to come and are also described in my previous work, *Folk Witchcraft: A Guide to Lore, Land, and the Familiar Spirit for the Solitary Practitioner*. Putting aside the purposes of divination and the seeking of magical knowledge via incantations and sigils revealed in spirit work, this "re-alignment" and redemptive process of liberating the dark parts of the soul is what we might call the greater work to be done.

Hopkins (1647) provides a historical sketch of several familiar spirits bonded to an early modern witch. His descriptions provide a helpful backdrop for discerning how our ancestors understood the nature and role of the familiar spirit in witch lore. In his account, the witch in question was served by several spirits with unique names and appearances:

i.   *Holt*, who came like a white kitling.

ii.   *Jarmara*, who came in like a fat spaniel, without any legs at all; she said she kept him fat, for she clapt her hand on her belly, and said he sucked good blood from her body.

iii.   *Vinegar Tom*, who was like a long-legged greyhound, with a head like an ox, with a long tail and broad eyes, who, when the discoverer spoke to and bade him go to the place provided for him and his angels, immediately transformed himself into the shape of a child four years old, without a head, and gave half a dozen turns about the house and vanished at the door.

iv.   *Sack and Sugar*, like a black rabbit.

v.   *Newes*, like a polecat.

From this description, we can see that, even hundreds of years in the past, familiar spirits were capable of changing forms, often assuming some variety of animal and human forms, but under no circumstances are they bound to those forms.

So far, we have described how we as modern witches seek to consort with spirits of the land, of the lore, and of the shadow in order to gain wisdom from the otherworld and to reunite with our kin in those precious moments. Spirit work is a crucial motivation for spirit flight; it is in moments of ekstasis, which is to say moments outside the body, that we step into our true nature. The freedom of the spirit journey allows us to reunite with ancient intelligences, experiencing first-hand the presence of beings only briefly described in our lore. The wisdom they share with us is precious, and their allyship endlessly valuable. Though we must always be careful in our choice of allies, it is better in witchcraft to risk the journey than to play the part of the coward.

In the witch's ecstatic rides among the hidden company, they may notice the significance of timing. Certain times of year prove more reliable than others in terms of achieving contact with powerful spirits and gaining transformative insights in one's craft. These times seem to align with shifting points in the seasons that have already been well-described in many volumes, most often those days and nights that have been called Candlemas (February 2nd), May Eve (April 30th), Lammas (August 1st), and All Hallows' Eve (October 31st). Drawn upon a wheel, these four points form an X and mark turning points in the seasons, and so some modern practitioners refer to them as cross-quarter days. Midsummer and Yule are also potent points for spirit work, though to a lesser degree than these. Although the New Age witch's calendar often includes Ostara and Mabon, there is very little fae-lore to confirm the significance of these dates from a folkloric perspective, and for this reason, most folk witches do not emphasize the equinoxes in their work. For help understanding the history of this lore and its significance to spirit flight, we turn again to Kirk's language from 1691:

> They [the hidden company] remove to other
> lodgings at the beginning of each quarter of the

year, so traveling till doomsday, being impotent of staying in one place, and finding some ease by so journeying and changing habitations. Their chameleon-like bodies swim in the air near the earth with bag and baggage; and at such revolutions of time, seers, or men of the second sight, have terrifying encounters with them, even on highways...

Kirk goes on to describe the common tradition among the Scottish and Irish of blessing one's cattle and belongings against attack by these "wandering tribes" of spirits.

The modern witch, however, need have no fear—only preparation, care, and a great deal of respect. (Remember, as fearsome as some of this company may be, they are our kin.) It is partially for this reason that witches often make offering before or after participating in spirit flight on these particular days of the year. A show of generosity and kindness will not only help to satiate the Old Ones, those masters of craft who have gone before and risen to the deific ranks, but it will also propitiate our familiars to guard us as we leave our bodies to join that ancient ride upon the deep.

On such excursions, the witch often finds that the form she inhabits upon leaving the body is different than the form she takes in waking life. *The Compendium Maleficarum* (1608), *The Malleus Maleficarum* (1487), and slews of other medieval and early modern texts describe the common understanding that witches went forth in spirit forms unlike their physical ones. This second body or spirit body is sometimes called the "hag" or "fetch." Its forms can vary immensely. One witch may experience her fetch as a long shadow; another may find that her fetch self takes on the form of a hare or toad. The shape assumed instinctively by the hag body reveals something, I believe, of the inner nature of the witch herself— those elements in which she finds shame or has experienced repression. That body desires to be liberated, and it is in the act of spirit flight that it takes its full form. With that liberation comes a kind of strength and power that one simply cannot experience in a physical body. The witch becomes capable of great feats of strength, of warding off enemies, of protecting loved ones, and indeed, of those dark acts of maleficium that have been called "hag-riding" or simply "riding."

The hag is in some ways an energetic expression of the dualistic nature of the witch himself. The fetch or hag body is the self of the wilderness, a reflection of an ancestral memory of hunter-gatherer ancestors, a forgotten piece of the human spirit that recalls its comfort with and mastery over the dark and wild. It is who we were. It is who we could have been. It is the shadow of us, the piece outside of civilization's walls and laws. The piece that has been rejected, forgotten, banished. The things we reject about ourselves are there. And fortunately for us as witches, all the power we will ever need is there, too.

Lessons at the Hidden Feast

One important reason witches undertake spirit flight is to participate in the spiritual communion that has been called the "witches' sabbat." Unlike the embodied sabbat rituals performed by many modern witches today, the event we are exploring now has no precise time or location. This etheric gathering has sometimes been called the spiritual or oneiric sabbat. We can understand it better as a state of consciousness and ecstasy, a visionary experience one achieves in spirit flight that affects a communion between the souls of witches across the world, the Old Ones who teach and govern our craft, and the many spirits who inhabit the otherworld.

One of the most important and repeated aspects of the otherworldly sabbat narrative is the sharing of nourishment in the form of a great feast. Scot (1584) paints a vivid portrayal of the feasting that early modern people believed took place at this secret gathering:

> ...after [the witches] have delicately banqueted with the Devil and the Lady of the Fairies; and have eaten up a fat ox, and emptied a butt of malmesie [a type of sweet wine], and a bin of bread at some nobleman's house in the dead of night, nothing is missed of all this in the morning. For the Lady Sibylla, Minerva, or Diana, with a golden rod, striketh the vessel and the bin, and they are fully replenished again. Yea, she causeth the bullock's bones to be brought and laid together upon the hide, and lappeth the four ends thereof together, laying her golden rod thereon; and then riseth up the bullock again in his former estate and condition: and yet, at their return home, they are like to starve for hunger...

This theme of an immense and extravagant banquet held in the spirit realm and overseen by the Devil and the Lady repeats itself throughout early modern and medieval witch-lore. The fact that the participants return home hungry indicates that the nourishment shared is of a spiritual nature, not a physical one. These witches, like witches today, were invited to participate in a ritual of spiritual nourishing that fortified their connection to the otherworld and cemented their bond with the denizens of that world. The guests at these feasts were described as including not only living witches, but the spirits of the dead, faeries, demons, imps, familiar spirits, and a diverse cast of otherworldly beings (Wilby, 2005). This shared meal, this shared sustenance, forges a bond that keeps us connected to our roots in Elphame, to our otherly nature.

Witches today feel called to attend this otherworldly convention. This call manifests itself as a deep yearning and urge that is difficult to define for those who have never experienced its like. It is evident in the spontaneous desire to disappear into the dark of the woods at night, to achieve access to some hidden dream that you cannot name. It is like the urge to rush outdoors to smell the scent of petrichor from a fresh rain. It is a homesickness, a lust bound up deep in the marrow of the soul to return to the heart of the otherness we feel at our core. The hunger for the hidden feast is more than a need for the spiritual sustenance available to us in that space. It is a soul-level alignment with the language and symbols of the sabbat; the feeling that we have some unspoken work yet to do, some purpose pulling us into the deep.

One of the most shrouded and poorly illuminated areas of our craft pertains not to grimoires, charms, deities, or any specific words or formulae of power (these things are not hidden; they are readily available to those with the skills to read and understand them), but to the source of our art itself. Where do our rites and methods originate? Who first spoke with the spirits catalogued in the grimoires? How did sorcerers first procure formulae like the infamous *askei kataskei* or *abaxacatabax?* The answers to these questions will lead us deeper into the nourishing dark of sabbat-craft and spirit work, for it is through these gates that witches are able to connect to what has been called the true Black Book, being the source of all magical knowledge, the hidden place where the roots of witches drink deep, wresting charms directly from the otherworld.

In practical terms, modern folk and traditional witches who observe the oneiric sabbat as part of their practice would describe the experience as invigorating. We come away from sabbatic ekstasis energized in our magics, and often with visionary experiences that can later be translated carefully into incantations, sigils, and recipes for our own personal craft. Words spoken to the witch can often be unpuzzled as anagrams or phonetic renderings of other phrases, resulting in barbarous words. Even short, seemingly nonsense phrases can be lengthened by adding the needed vowels, resulting in beautifully ornate incantations. Images shown to the witch can be translated into sigils by drawing their basic shapes and lines repeatedly, reducing the visual form down to its most basic shape composed of the fewest lines possible. The exercises that follow in this book will help new witches develop the necessary skills of sight to procure charms in all of

the ways described here. These and other processes have and are still being used by witches today to derive an ever-flowing curriculum of magical arts, an endless, etheric grimoire of learning that never ceases to provide new charms and insights to those willing to seek and to learn.

On a higher level, our sabbat preserves a treasure trove of lessons embedded in the tropes and metaphors with which witches continue to engage. The invisible spirit flight by night to attend the lessons of the Old Ones and participate in the hidden feast is more than the seeking of power and knowledge for living witches. Its experience is a living, actualized embodiment of principles and concepts that are rooted in the animist roots of witchcraft. Though folk witches like myself are non-dogmatic in nature and tend to shun rules, these "themes" emerge so frequently that one cannot help but appreciate them after years and years of practice. These principles extend their reach beyond the oneiric sabbat to influence the ways witches act and believe in day-to-day life, reaffirming certain values we inevitably and naturally share. Though sabbatic experiences may differ significantly by the heritage and locale of the individual witch, the following are generally present:

i. The union of the witch with flora and with fauna. The spiritual location experienced by most witches in sabbatic ekstasis is a hidden, natural scene—a secluded spot deep in the woods, the pinnacle of a mountain, the bottom of the ocean, the beaches of a sandy isle. The spirits who attend these rites, the familiars of other witches in attendance, and indeed even the form of the witch's fetch itself may take an animal form either in whole or in part. The Devil, who may also be understood as the King of Elphame, is often experienced as being part man and part black goat, horse, or stag. At this collective ritual of learning and feasting, all are welcome at the table. The witch is in no way positioned as superior to the animal and plant spirits in attendance. All at the gathering are on equal footing. This principle reminds us that the worlds of flora and fauna do not exist for our pleasure and amusement or for our sole nourishment; we are participants in an elegant tapestry, an interdependence that calls us to respect other life forms on this planet instead of subjugating and enslaving them to our wills.

ii. The union of the living and the dead. At the table of the sabbat, there is no division between those spirits who possess living bodies on earth and those who have departed to the afterlife. In fact, the faeries who are frequently depicted in the lore as attending the witches' sabbat can also be understood as the ancient ancestors of those in attendance. The appearance of these spirits near prehistoric burial mounds and the identification of "elf darts" with ancient arrowhead relics testify to the faery faith as a kind of ancestor veneration lost to recent memory, a survived form of what has been called a "cult of the dead." In attending the sabbat with these beings, we modern witches are offered a lesson: that the dead were once just as we are now, and that time, in the language of the spirit, does not exist. To have existed once, even in a life thousands of years ago, is to exist always. In the otherworld, nothing is lost, for memory is long indeed. In our understanding of this fact, we are called to live fully and to accept our eventual death, viewing it as a contingency of our current life rather than a horrible surprise that would steal our living bodies (which were never truly ours to begin with).

iii. The interdependence of all life through cyclical consumption. The feasting that takes place in the fields of spirit is emblematic of the cycles of predation and consumption that make up the natural world. In the famous Gundestrup cauldron, we see a representation of this balance. A figure in a horned headdress, representing perhaps an early Celtic shaman convening with the spirit world, sits in a meditative pose between imagery representing a variety of predators, prey animals, and plant forms. In one hand, they hold a torc, and in the other, a serpent. Many of the creatures depicted in this metalwork are connected by complex food cycles and ecosystems. Like the pack of wolves hunting the rabbit, we human beings sustain our bodies by drawing life from other organisms, both plant and animal. Even the act of breathing itself draws chemical nourishment from the air around us, consuming atoms in the process. At the end of our lives, our bodies are returned to the plant world to be devoured and transformed into more nourishment yet. By participating in the ceremonial feast of the spirit, witches are called to responsible, mindful consumption, understanding that, though it is necessary to take some life in order to live, we can choose to do so thoughtfully and sustainably, in recognition of the greater cycle of the feast.

iv. The triumph of joy and pleasure over shame and pain.
In both our lore and the living continuum of our ecstatic experiences, witches describe dancing and revelry at the sabbat, including sexual and sensual acts. Though the early modern descriptions are most certainly exaggerated by the influence of witch-hunters to paint a more (by their minds) perverse picture, it is nonetheless the case that many witches today experience sensual pleasures at the oneiric sabbat. These experiences are not always penetrative or even overtly sexual; often, witches describe dancing naked with others, participating in cheeky games, and even simple touching and kissing with the spirits of other witches, imps, familiars, faeries, or even the Old Ones themselves, usually the Devil and the Queen of Elphame. For practitioners who have experienced sexual trauma or disassociation with their physical bodies, the spiritual ecstasies of the sabbat can provide a path to healing. Because of the nature of the oneiric sabbat, which is attended in spirit and not in body, these acts are always consensual, enjoyable to all involved, and conducted in a spirit of playfulness and frivolity, offering a window for us as modern witches to release, even for a moment, the hatred the modern world instills in us for our bodies. We are allowed for a moment to be sacred in our pleasures, to release shame, and to enjoy ourselves unapologetically. The joys of sex, food, drink, and

merriment are not distractions from spiritual truth and attainment; as witches, we believe that humans are, in fact, meant to feel *good* in our bodies. Starving ourselves of joy and pleasure will not bring a reward in some future world. The world is here, and it is now. Likewise, we recognize in this truth that every life is equally deserving of its own joys and pleasures, that the cost of our own pleasures cannot be pain to another. Slavery, cruelty, abuse, and puritanism will never bring us the ecstasy we truly seek at our core since these things disrupt the harmony of the sabbat.

v. The integration of divided spiritual worlds through the opening of gates. At the sabbat, beings are called forth from many places. We have already discussed the diverse spiritual presences in attendance at the hidden feast—spirits of flora and fauna, local land spirits, faeries, familiars, imps, the dead—and each of these beings come to and depart from the sabbat to their own abode. Sometimes, the charms and incantations shared with us at this spiritual gathering are designed, in part, to help us open gates and better understand the spirits who dwell on the other side of them. This principle is evident in the gate-opening charm I have included and described in my previous book, *Folk Witchcraft*:

> One, two, three, and four;
> The Old Ones knock upon the door.

Welcome them from floor to roof.
Drink to them in a horse's hoof.
Call the cat, the toad, the bran.
Come to the feast, all ye who can.
One, two, three, and four:
The Old Ones are here, so no more.

Note that this version refers to the Old Ones as opposed to the Devil, the name used in the original early modern Welsh version. This adaptation is not from fear of calling on "the Devil" (since we know that the folkloric Devil of our craft is quite different from the "Devil" of the bible), but for easier usage by witches who align with a variety of heritage-based teaching spirits. Regardless, we see here in this incantation the opening of a gate to affect the mingling of the witch's spirit with the Old Ones and several animal spirits. While the cosmology of the Abrahamic religions teaches that separate worlds exist for different spirits, an imposed order overseen by a single ruler and creator, witches recognize a diversity and pluralism in the spiritual landscape. "Good" and "evil" are unhelpful concepts for us. A benevolent spirit may appear in an unusual or frightening form, and a malicious one in the guise of an angel. The only way we are to gain knowledge and power in our art is to open those doors, to face the beings that lie beyond with full confidence in ourselves, and to recognize that we are all already connected.

Moreover, we are called by the communal

nature of the sabbat to recognize that, historically, humans in the traditions of ceremonial magic have enslaved and abused spirits of the otherworld, naming them "demons" and demanding that they deliver us wealth, knowledge, and influence, as if the otherworld were merely a piggy bank to serve human desires. Many folk and traditional witches open gates at the spiritual sabbat to honor our kinship with those beings and to reject the hierarchical cosmologies of the Abrahamic faiths. In do doing, a secret truth is revealed: just as we conjure spirits from the otherworld to aid in our rites, so are *we* conjured by *them* to attend the spiritual rites of that hidden company.

vi. The empowerment of the witch through the embrace of the fearsome dark. In this sixth principle, we come to one of the most difficult lessons in old craft. Witchcraft is not safe, and it is not a path for the weak of mind or spirit. There are dark truths kept in the deep crags of the otherworld. In our lore, we read tales of witches encountering horrifying and threatening figures that would prevent them from traveling by means of spirit flight. Isobel Gowdie described great bull-like creatures that prowled the underground caverns leading to the meeting place of witches (Wilby, 2010). Regardless of the forms we witness in the shadow, it is only by facing that darkness that we are able to make progress in our craft and build what we might call the equivalent of spiritual "muscle." In embarking upon spirit flight, particularly for those new to the practice, it is common to experience a challenge from shadow figures. While many inexperienced witches jump to the conclusion that they are being assaulted by a malevolent spirit, the truth is usually simpler. When we begin to enter the otherworld in our new spiritual form, we encounter phantoms of our own barriers, our own created thoughtforms, that we designed long ago to hold us back. In a world that fears magic and hates the shadow, many of us build these constructs ourselves at a young age in order to keep us from embarking too far upon the deep. These are the ghosts of our own fear, our own unwillingness to accept our otherness. They are a manifestation of self-loathing that has been ingrained in the witch, a demonization of self. If we are able to face them as part of ourselves and make the journey, other darknesses prove easier. We can accept that death and predation are a part of life. We can accept that the natural world that is the source of our craft's animistic roots is indeed both dark and light at once. In embracing the dark, we reject the idea of an unbalanced existence, of being all-kind or all-cruel, and recognize that wholeness means accepting our capacity for both so that we might truly choose for ourselves and be free.

If we are bold enough to receive the calling

of the witches' sabbat and to answer it, we learn that there is more at stake here than the learning of charms and the alignment with the otherworldly powers that are our source. We are called by these principles of communion and freedom to manifest the sabbat here on earth. We do this spiritually in all the ways we have previously described, and we do it physically by living a life informed by these lessons, guided by them, ever reaching for a greater understanding of our responsibilities and impact as powerful beings in this world.

Preparations—and an Invitation

As an animist spiritual practice, folk witchcraft is challenging not in its complexity, but in its simplicity. It asks us to approach the world very plainly in an experiential, phenomenological way that contradicts empirical thought. Some of the rituals and charms in this book will ask you to do the same.

If you are unsure about your readiness for the work described in this book, try the following exercises first. They will offer you the necessary background of basic practice to begin experimenting with the individual gates described in the sections that follow.

Speaking with the Moon

Walk outside at night, and look at the moon. See her. Do not look for your own understanding of what "the moon" means--her measurements, her history, her place in science and in symbolism. Do not look for the moon in concept or imagination; she isn't there. Look at the moon *herself*. See her the way she chooses to be seen on this night, right now, by you alone. See her plainly, without preconception, the way countless ancient peoples saw her. See her casting her pale glow. See the ring around her. Notice her shape, her details.

Choose to believe, for just a moment, that the moon doesn't need humans to name her, measure her gravitational field, or define her existence in any way. Look at the moon. She is sufficient unto herself. She exists without words or symbols to represent her. She is there. Just there. You and the moon are together in this wondrous moment. You have both arrived here, and so here you are, basking in the presence of one other.

Now, allow yourself to accept, if just for a moment, that the moon is gazing back at you. And why not? If you can look at the moon, why shouldn't the moon look back at you? Why shouldn't she see and hear you? Suspend your empirical mind with its narcissistic human logic. The moon isn't in your mind. No. She's here, with you. What you see and hear and feel is real. Your moment alone with the moon is real.

Speak to the moon. Actually speak to her. Do not speak merely to yourself with her as an audience. Do not prattle on, waxing poetic with your ideas of what the moon means and represents. Be present. Look at the moon. Speak to the moon with the full expectation that she can hear you. What would you say to her? What would you ask her? Know that she will answer you, not with human words, but with a breeze against the nearby trees, a firefly, a shift of cloud. Converse with the moon, and learn to see. Learn to listen. Acts of real magic can be surprisingly simple.

Awakening the Witch-sight

Before one can begin a regular practice of spirit flight, it is necessary to gain control of the otherworldly senses. After all, how can we begin to perceive in etheric travels outside the physical body before we can sense the spiritual currents at work in our immediate proximity?

Many witches possess innate visionary skills. You may have sensed or seen spirits in the past—often as a shadow in your peripheral vision or an apparition or voice in those states between waking and dreaming. As a child, I frequently experienced spiritual visitors in the middle of the night, to such an extent that I felt swarmed by them. It would take many years for me to understand how to control the sight. Without control, witch-sight overwhelms our senses at full blast with little or no warning, like a radio turned on at maximum volume in the middle of the night or while driving on the interstate. All witches must learn how to engage and disengage this sense so that they can function in the world without unwelcome interruption.

What we are calling "witch-sight" is actually a shift in consciousness. The otherworldly consciousness we use to perceive and interact with spiritual beings is a second set of senses that have nothing to do with the senses used by our mundane consciousness. We can control our active form of consciousness with ritual practices that are repeated over time so that certain actions or words become a kind of password, a stimulus that triggers the shift within us when we *want* it to happen.

Whether you are still developing your sight or learning to control it, begin with the following simple ritual. You will only need a candle and a quiet place to work.

Sit comfortably on the floor in a dark room (yes, it needs to be dark; darkness allows us to drown out mundane consciousness so that we can sense more subtle presences) with a single candle lit near you. Allow yourself to play with the shadows made by the candlelight. Pass your hands before and behind the candle flame (being careful not to burn yourself, of course). Watch the shadows stretch across the walls of the room. Close your eyes, and pass your hand between the candle and yourself. Let the shadows wash over your eyelids like waves of darkness. Notice the difference between these two darknesses. Even with the eyes closed, what we call darkness is really just dampened light. When our eyes close under the additional darkness of a shadow, we experience a deeper dark.

Now, breathe deeply, and relax your body. Allow yourself to sway rhythmically with the shadows passing over your eyelids. Feel the shadows passing over you as a physical thing, almost a current of wind, something you can feel not with your skin, but with some other, hidden sense. Continue to move with your breaths, long and slow.

You may feel moved to stretch your arms or bend your neck this way or that; if so, abandon your shadow-play and move as desired. Do not be surprised if you feel a sense of ecstasy in your movements. Because we deny our nonphysical senses in our daily lives, there is a pleasure in stepping into them again, like slipping into a warm bath. You are allowing yourself to *feel* the currents of the unseen world, responding to their movements with your nerve endings. You are unshackling a part of you that has been bound and gagged for some time. Do not be alarmed if you are moved to strange breathing patterns, utterances, and contortions. You are learning to be both in and out of your body at once, and the response from your nervous system may feel strange.

If you possess such aptitudes, you may hear voices or see visions as you continue to move and breathe in the dark. If not, that is fine. Simply allow yourself to careen on the ecstasy of the shadow. After repeated sessions, the sight will come—in whatever manner you possess it, it will come. If you sense something unpleasant, either an entity or an echo from the past that disturbs you, simply exhale deeply, emptying your lungs of all air, and place your two hands flat upon the floor in a firm gesture. This will arrest your etheric perceptions and bind them to your physical form once more.

As you continue to build your powers of witch-sight and otherworldly perception, remember the heart of this lesson: your experience of the world around you, your very consciousness, is not a fixed or solid thing. It is malleable, and you have the power to bend it. You can open that door within yourself, and you can close it again—as surely as an instrument can be tuned and played, then put away in its case when the song is done.

Empowering the Fetch or Hag-body

It is not enough to claim to have power in the otherworld. You must *know* it. Without power, one is vulnerable in the spirit realm. Like the physical world, there are predators and prey, and so it is necessary to develop muscle, to build strength and control. A witch is not a victim or a morsel for hungry entities in the otherworld; we are the living descendants of the Old Ones, of those dread powers who have been called by many names: Hecate, Pan, Diana, Medea, Cernunnos, Herne, Lilith, Cain, Lucifer, and even the Devil himself. To those outside of our craft, some of these names are fearful, but we know a different side of them. To the witch, these are parents, teachers, guides, mentors, and kin. Imagine their reaction to a witch who cowers before a spider, who jumps at a shadow. No, if we are to claim the legacy of witchcraft, we must become strong. We must proceed in all of our craft with the full knowledge that *we* are the ones to be feared in the otherworld—our true home, our place of power.

It is the need for strength that necessitates the use of the fetch or hag body, which is essentially the spirit body altered and controlled under the force of the witch's own magical will. Regardless of the limitations of the physical body—whether due to age, size, or ability—the etheric body is unbound by matter and can be compelled to transmogrification by simple, lesser arts.

Begin once more in a dark room with a single candle, but this time, place the candle behind you (at a safe distance so as not to burn yourself). Gaze upon your shadow's form on the wall. Watch how it mirrors your own movement. Using your powers of witch-sight, begin to notice the details behind the shadow. What does its face look like? Its hands? Its feet? How is it like and unlike your own physical form? Realize that the shadow you see before you is merely the physical counterpart of the shadow cast in the otherworld. Do not be afraid if your hag possesses features you associate with hunter/predator animals. It may have scales, horns, talons, or any combination of fearful features. This is no cause for alarm; in fact, like any creature in nature, your fetch may instinctively assume a form with natural self-defense features. All living things have the right to defend themselves, and because your fetch is malleable, it may assume forms that *you* associate with danger. This is well and good, for it means you will have greater defense in the otherworld. As you continue to meditate upon your fetch's characteristics, you may also wish to name it so that it may be called upon when needed. Any name will do, so long as it evokes for you the nature of the form you have identified in your fetch.

At this point, you will need a pendulum. This can be a purchased pendulum or one you have made yourself by tying a ring onto the end of a length of thread. There is a long history of constructing pendulums this way in folk craft, so there is no need to buy a pendulum if you do not already own one.

Hold the thread of the pendulum in your dominant hand, allowing the weight at the end to hang still. Gaze softly at the pendulum's weighted

end with your eyes half-closed, and *see* your shadow's hand moving the pendulum counterclockwise. Focus all your intention on it, but do not move your arm to make it so. It is only your fetch that moves the pendulum. It should feel very easy and natural. Allow the image of the pendulum spinning to consume your mind's eye as you gaze upon it. Be patient with yourself, and allow yourself more than one try if needed. If you have had success with the previous rite, you may be surprised at how quickly your fetch, through the subtle manipulation of the body's invisible rhythms, is able to cause the pendulum to move.

When you are satisfied, put away the pendulum, and remember this lesson: all of the strength you will need is there already. Yes, the otherworld is not without its dark entities, but they pale in comparison to the dark powers of our own ancestors. Witches are kind, careful, and respectful in our spirit work because we *choose* to be. We show good manners because we *choose* to do so. Fear is only useful until it has no more use.

Calling the Familiar Spirit

Allies are incredibly helpful in spirit work. They can spell the difference between safe passage through the otherworld and dangerous excursions that risk harm to our spiritual beings and psyches. Before embarking upon spirit flight, it is recommended that any witch acquire at least one decent familiar spirit.

Unlike the fetch or hag, the familiar spirit is not a reflection of the practitioner; it is a separate entity that has bound itself in communion with the witch in exchange for offerings or energy or sometimes simply out of love. During the witch's mundane hours of work or chores or reading novels, the familiar spirit attends to its own affairs. It is not a djinn trapped in a bottle or a pet kept on a leash. The sacred dwellings we build for familiar spirits are used only at the spirit's pleasure. It is important that the witch allow the familiar spirit full autonomy and freedom; these things are necessary to any healthy, trusting relationship, and spirits are no different. One has only to glimpse at renaissance grimoires to realize that the history of magical practice is full of spirit evocations that involve imprisoning, torturing, or humiliating the conjured spirit in order for the magician to achieve some petty wish fulfillment. This is cruel and barbaric to any serious practitioner with a shred of empathy, and it should be as disgusting to witches as it is to our kin in the otherworld.

Instead of compelling spirits, witches will achieve lasting growth in their craft by building relationships of trust, honesty, and generosity. This does take time, but it is the only way *true* loyalty can be built. The basic process consists of opening communication, making repeated offerings, ensuring safe boundaries, and allowing the spirit to be the first to offer the bond. After all, humans have mistreated and abused them for hundreds of years. Trusting humans has not, historically speaking, ended well for spirits, and so it will take kindness and more than a little bit of patience to acquire a familiar.

The benefits of a familiar are impossible to count, but of all of these, the most priceless is perhaps the ability to conduct spirit flight with a guardian to stand sentinel beside you on the journey. Although the fetch provides a great deal of power if spiritual danger arises, its use requires active concentration and effort on the part of the witch. Having a decent familiar allows the witch to fend off pests without expending any energy of her own, like having a high-functioning immune system. In addition to this priceless gain, the familiar spirit can offer the witch tutelage in those magical arts that pertain to its nature, revealing charms, sigils, and formulae as the practitioner grows in her craft. In exchange, the witch offers the spirit vital sustenance in the form of offerings that usually consist of fumigation, praise, and loving attention.

Begin with the spirit of a plant or animal that thrives in your own region. It should be something you have seen before multiple times. Do not overlook obvious choices like plantain, ragweed, crickets, and birds because you feel you deserve a rare familiar like a serpent, crocodile, or bat. You may be surprised to learn that snakes are incredibly delicate and vulnerable creatures, basically a length of soft flesh with a mouth on one end. On the other hand, plantain, although it is only a common weed, can endure being trampled over and over and still flower. It thrives even in adversity, and it grows almost anywhere. Be open to surprises, and once you decide upon a plant or animal, set out to observe it as closely as you can over a series of several days. Commit its form and movements to memory. Learn everything you can about it. Introduce yourself, and speak your intentions. If the creature is an animal, you may do this from a distance so as not to frighten it. Leave small offerings of water, fruit, nuts, or whatever its pleasure may be.

After you have done this for at least three sessions, return to a dark room with a single candle lit, like in the previous exercises. Let your witch-sight come alive, using the previous shadow-play exercise if needed. Call to the spirit using simple words of pure intention, such as the following:

Spirit of ____, I conjure you.
Come, spirit of ____, by and by.

If it is your pleasure to use Latinate charms (since the unique sounds of Latin and their historical association with folk craft do temper the atmosphere of ritual), feel free to use the following:

Coniuro te, spiritus creaturae.

You may wish to repeat your incantation as a chant as you fall into a comfortable rhythm, allowing your body to rock back and forth. Recall the feeling of the shadow play exercises, and allow yourself to unbind your sight again. Allow that wave of release to wash over you as you call to the spirit. Permit yourself to perceive the spirit in subtle ways: perhaps as a shadow in the corner of the room, as a sense of heat or cold, as a tingling in your skin, as an unexplained sound or a flicker of candlelight.

Close your eyes, and ask the spirit to reveal itself to you. Explain that you call to it only with affection, that you ask nothing, that you wish only to perceive it and to listen and see what it chooses to show you. Offer an incense of mugwort or some pleasant floral fumigation; incense is a traditional gift to spirits. Be receptive, passive, and polite. Try to remember any images, words, or numbers you are shown in your session with the spirit; these can later be translated into a name and sigil by following your growing intuition and powers of witch-sight. In the future, the name and sigil can be utilized to call to the spirit more effectively. These secrets should never be shared with anyone unless the spirit gives you clear permission to do so, but even then, it is ill-advised. Those who learn the name and properties of a spirit may (if they possess the necessary skills) summon it, contain it, sap its strength, or harm it.

Once you have succeeded in conjuring the spirit several times, it will either offer to bind itself to you as a familiar, or it will not. It is important that the choice be made by the spirit and the spirit alone. If it chooses you, you will know without any doubt that it is so. If you accept, you will be entering into an agreement of sorts, and certain things will be expected of you.

Know that the relationship between a witch and her familiar must be maintained just like any relationship in this world. A spirit bottle, box, or some other decorated dwelling should be created and placed on your altar or in a location sacred to your practice so that the spirit has a place to rest and recuperate at its pleasure. Regular offerings will be expected. Kindness and respect will always be required. With regular care and dedication over time, the relationship between the familiar and the witch grows to one of both trust and love.

Opening the Crossroads

While much of Wicca and ceremonial magic involves the erecting of protective magical barriers, the folk witch does not require their use.

We prefer to rely on the defensive powers of our familiar spirits, our ancestral Old Ones, and our fetch. Though compasses, rings, or circles are sometimes conjured in order to sanctify a space for practice, the operative principle is not magical defense, but the opening of a door between worlds in order to extend an invitation. The ring or compass of our art is a passage, not a wall.

While the circle or ring is an old custom well-attested in the grimoire tradition, I recommend that new folk witches begin with a crossroads. This ancient symbol of intersection has long been associated with otherworldly encounter and the art of witches. It is here that the folkloric Devil offers a deal. It is here that Hecate, an ancient witch-queen, Our Lady of the Crossroads, maintains her vigil in her role as Kleidouchos (keeper of keys). Modern witches can utilize this potent reservoir of power in order to affect the opening of gates between worlds with great reliability.

Thankfully, we need not hazard a busy intersection in order to perform this work. If you are lucky enough to live in the country, it is of course helpful to visit an actual crossroads, perhaps leaving a small offering for the spirits who frequent there, but most modern-day crossroads, despite the romanticizing claims of many books, are not usually very conducive to the concentration necessary in effective spirit work. Instead, the practitioner can open a symbolic crossroads through specific ritual technique.

Begin seated on the floor in a dark room. Again, a single lit candle can be used so that you are not operating in total blindness. If necessary, use the shadow-play exercise to engage your otherworldly senses. (By now you are no doubt realizing one of the secrets to regular, effective spirit work practice; the lighting of a single candle in a darkened room acts as a trigger for your witch-sight, allowing you to awaken that hidden part of yourself at will.) With your index finger, trace an X upon the floor, and speak your intention to open a way between the worlds. It is important that you *see* the lines as you trace them, almost as if your finger were burning the marks into the floor. If you don't mind cleaning up afterwards, you can lay the X using flour or with chalk. You may, if you wish, utilize the following incantation, derived from Welsh witch-lore:

> *One, two, three, and four.*
> *The Old Ones knock upon the door.*
> *Welcome them from floor to roof.*
> *Drink to them in a horse's hoof.*
> *Call the cat, the toad, the bran.*
> *Come to the feast, all ye who can.*
> *One, two, three, and four.*
> *The Old Ones are here, so no more.*

At this point, it is helpful to knock three times upon the center of the X. Doing so alerts those on the other side that you have opened a door to their world. It is both good etiquette and a signal to the dread powers that govern our art that you are one of their own, ready to make the crossing.

The geometric configuration of the crossroads may be "pulled open" via your witch-sight in order to render the passage into a tunnel (see figure). As you form this gesture with your hands, focus on *seeing* the lines you traced upon the floor pull open as well, forming a vacuum in the center of the X you formed before. If done properly, you will sense a slight coolness, like the air from an underground cave. You may also feel a very delicate pull, like the pressure released when opening a window in a stagnant, sealed room.

To cross through this tunnel, you will need to move your spirit out of your physical body. Call to your fetch by its name, and feel your form shift into its likeness. This may take some time on the first try. One of the secrets to successfully departing the body is *not trying too hard*. It should feel like a pleasurable release, not a strain; it is like unclenching a muscle that you didn't know was being flexed. At first, you may feel like a double-exposure photograph, the image of your fetch overlapping with the image of your physical self. Pay it no mind. Begin to slowly practice moving your spirit in fetch form without moving your

body. Once you are able, step away from your physical form, and look back on your body. Do not be surprised if you are still able to sense your physical body as well; this is not a barrier to practice, and any distraction it poses will dissipate as you gain experience with embodying your fetch-form. When you are ready, climb down through the tunnel you have created.

What you experience in the otherworld is for you and you alone. It is a personal encounter with the Old Ones, with the ancestors of our craft, with your own familiar and local spirits. In the beginning, the witch should focus on awakening the senses fully on the other side of the gate, perhaps by exploring the following questions:

- *What does the air feel like? Is it cool or warm, dry or moist? Is the air still? Is there a gentle wind? A blustering gale?*

- *What do you smell? Smoke? Wet earth? Petrichor (the chemical released by rain hitting soil)? Honeysuckle? Pine? The dung of livestock? The salt of the sea?*

- *What do you hear? The crackle of a fire in the distance? The sound of rain pelting rock? The churn of the sea? The shifting of sand? Birds? Crickets? Toads? Are there voices calling on the wind? What do they say?*

- *If there is solid ground, what is its composition? Is it a pebbled beach? A weedy path overgrown with briars? A grassy hill?*

- *Lastly, what do you see? Darkness or fog may conceal things from you, but gaze carefully. Is there a light in the distance? A shifting form? Who or what waits for you there, beyond the edge of your vision?*

This ritual is effective, but it is but one way to open a gate between worlds. The thirteen chapters that follow will offer additional gates with additional wisdom to be gained from each.

~ 🖝 ~

Now I invite you, dear reader, to open these thirteen doors to your own craft, to your own power. I invite you to the hidden company and to the ecstasy of the spirit. For those with the aptitude to master these skills, the way is open. I offer these thirteen gates not as prescriptive rituals, but as currents of symbol and art that may be shaped by the individual practitioner in much the same way any instrument may bend a note. May you tread upon the deep with kindness and respect, and may the lessons you find there lead you to greater wisdom and meaning in your life.

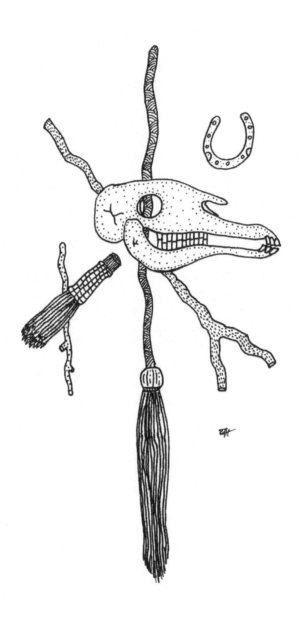

Via Equarum

In a dark room, a single candle casts its glow upon the floor. Its light illuminates the pale, horned skull of a goat between two bundles of lavender, an apple, and a glass of red wine. This is the altar: substance of bone and of field, of flora and fauna, laid together with the offerings to be made after the work is done.

The witch is seated before these items in silence, meditating upon her purpose this night, focusing her intentions before beginning the rite at hand. Silently, she focuses on seeing without her eyes, conjuring her witch sight so that she may be able to perceive the subtle currents that will churn in the working that is to come. She gazes with her witch eyes at the dark of the room surrounding her. Shadows dance across the goat skull as she passes her hand over the candle, calling to the Old Ones, those beautiful, wise, and terrible ancient spirits who rule over the work of witches.

Mother and father of my art,
Teachers and guides on the path,

> *Bless this gate between the worlds.*
> *Be with me on this night.*
> *Io Regina Pigmeorum.* [*]
> *Io Dominus Umbrarum.*

She feels her call resound in the deep, echoing into the hidden places of the otherworld. The candle flickers for but a moment. The Old Ones are here.

The witch reaches behind her for one of her most trusted tools: a length of wood split into two branches at the end, in the shape of a Y—her stang, her staff of art, and on this night, in this ritual, her steed, one that will carry her forth into the currents of the otherworld like a crow on a cool breeze, like a salmon disappearing into dark waters. With a centering breath, she stands the staff upright, leaning her weight upon it by grabbing the two prongs on its end with her hands.

> *Famulus—I conjure you.*
> *Mossbelly, my faithful familiar,*
> *I conjure your spirit into this vessel*
> *of wood and art*
> *that you might convey me to the otherworld*
> *thither by night, by air, and by the dark.*

With her witch-sight, she sees the familiar form of her ally—a toad with moss growing on its back. She watches it climb the staff on which she leans, watches as its

---

[*] This appellation of Our Lady is attested in the works of William Lilly in the mid-1600s, loosely rendered as "Dark Queen."

amphibious form melds into the wood. As she squeezes the two ends of her staff, she can feel Mossbelly's heart beating within it now, ready for the flight. She begins the chant slowly, using the old words:

> Horse and hattock.
> Horse and go.
> Horse and pellatis.
> Ho, ho.[*]

As she continues her rhythmic chant, she feels her spirit loosen from her form, like a window being opened in an air-tight room. She bears her weight more and more upon the staff she holds, and with her spirit sight, perceives that she is no longer bearing down upon the ground.

She can hear the chant faster now, but it does not come from her own mouth. It comes from her body, which she can see sitting below her in the room. Above her head, instead of the ceiling of the room, she can see the vast, moonlit sky, clouds rushing across its onyx black. As she rises, the witch feels her freedom in this form. As she careens off into the churning winds, she feels strong and prepared for the journey, blessed by the Old Ones, by her familiar, by the moon and stars themselves.

---

[*] A verbal charm described by Scottish witch Isobel Gowdie in 1662. "Horse and hattock" was considered in the folklore of the time to be what faeries cried out before going invisible and disappearing into the otherworld at the presence of a mortal. A "hattock" is thought to mean a small hat.

~ 🖎 ~

The passage above offers but one example among many of the ways modern folk witches draw on the lore and legacy of spirit flight in the use of broom and staff as charmed vehicle. The image of the witch gliding across the night sky astride her broom is so ubiquitous in popular culture that this trope is recognized across the western world. Like many such images, though, it is sourced part in fact and part in misconception. While witches continue to utilize brooms as an aid to spirit flight, the same purpose may in truth be served by sticks, staves, and pitchforks.

One of the most famous historic references for this concept comes from the trial of Alice Kyteler in 1324. It was claimed that investigators found in her house "a pipe of ointment, wherewith she greased a staff upon which she ambled and galloped through thicke and thin" (Seymour, 1913). Elsewhere, in the *Compendium Maleficarum*, we find reference to the devil empowering a staff with the power of aiding the witch in traveling long distances upon the air (Guazzo, 1608). These bits of lore were the early beginnings of what would become an overwhelmingly popular folk belief surrounding the activities of witches.

In order to better understand the progression of this belief, we must turn to the lore and traditions of the hobby horse of Western Europe. "Hobby horse" is a term used by academics to refer to a diverse array of folk traditions involving a stand-in for a horse in seasonal and agricultural festivals. This symbolic horse can be made of sticks, fabric, dried stalks, and can at times even involve the actual skull of a horse placed on the end of a rod. This is the case in the example set by the Welsh tradition of the Mari Lwyd or "grey mare." The horse skull fixed on the end of a rod is taken across the town, stopping at residences along the way in its ritual procession. Walker (2008) suggests that the tradition of the grey mare is indicative of a crossing or passage between the old and the new, particularly the passage of time since this festival is held in the cold of winter as a part of larger wassailing traditions.

In turning again to the *Abramelin* text of the 14-1600s, we find a reference to witches leaping about the fields on broomsticks, showing the crops "how high to grow." There is much to be said regarding the symbolic flight of witches around the cross-quarter days of the year and the agricultural shifts in the land itself among those who grow food and care for animals. The call to attend the hidden feast on these days is itself no coincidence, and modern witches who perform transvective rites at these times can experience for themselves the attunement to the growth cycles of the land around them.

Although much has been made of the idea that witches anoint staves and brooms with nightshade ointments and then insert them into their orifices to experience hallucinatory flight, this idea is flawed at a most basic level; speaking as a witch who carefully crafts and uses nightshades in my practice, the amount of tropane alkaloids necessary to experience such a high would be devastating if inserted into the body. This bit of fakelore can be attributed to our modern tendency to connect anything spiritual or magical to a mere chemical process, to reduce all things to empirical science and the mere sum of their parts. Rather, from existing historical descriptions, we see a clear connection between the hobby horse, the flight of witches, and the agricultural cycles that were important to our ancestors. Hobby horse folk traditions like these were once a popular and common occurrence in many parts of the world.

It does not take an academic to deduce the connection here for us as modern witches. Our animist ancestors sought to connect and interact with the spirits of plants and animals on which they relied for survival, a basic underlying principle of animism across the world. For them, agriculture was crucial. The besom (or broom), then, becomes two things at once: a staff resembling the familiar hobby horse form for conjuring the spirit horse, and a dried, tufted end representing the world of flora and the vegetation on which humans relied.

The use of a spirit horse in animism is an ancient and lasting practice—and for good reason. The horse represents one of the most ancient and impactful alliances between humans and the animal world, a pact made by our ancestors with a penchant for charming wild creatures, and one that is actually quite magical.

This image of the witch mounting the spirit steed is evocative of such a diverse tapestry of myth that it is chiseled in our tales of the Old Ones who rule the otherworld. This practice connects us to the ancient image of the sorcerer's god Odin on his eight-legged horse Sleipnir, riding across the skies as he leads the Wild Hunt; to Herne the Hunter who leaps and bounds across Windsor Forest on his steed to haunt his lands, his antlers rattling against the dry October leaves; to the chariot of the lunar goddess Selene, drawn across the night sky by her bulls; to Thor, who traveled about the land with the aid of his chariot drawn by two magical goats who could not die, Tanngrisnir and Tanngnojostr. In the symbolic vehicle of the broom, staff, and stang, we follow the pattern set by the Old Ones and participate in the living tradition of spirit flight ourselves.

In the broom (or besom, if one prefers the Old English word), we see a totemized human or spirit figure embedded in an everyday object that would have been available to our ancestors without the need to purchase special tools. Held or propped upside-down, the broom's bristles form a head of hair at the top of its staff length. It is not difficult to imagine how such a prop could become a fetish representing a spirit that one wishes to honor.

Nor is it difficult to imagine how the broom can become a stand-in for the target of magical acts. In witch-lore, we have inherited numerous tales of victims being ridden like horses, often experiencing this torment as a nightmare and waking to find themselves at home in their beds, exhausted as if having sprinted all night long (Davis, 1975). A witch interested in this form of maleficium might begin by collecting an item belonging to the victim to be tied to the broom or staff with the thread. If such an item is not available, the broom can also be conjured as simulacrum using a sigilized form of the victim's name. In this way, the spirit of the intended party can be called into the broom much like the familiar can be, though a witch who rides her familiar of course affords her companion a great deal more care and respect than a hag-ridden victim.

The stang featured in the narrative at the beginning of this chapter—a staff with a forked or pronged end—is a fairly modern tool in witchcraft, though it does in many ways resemble some older forms of distaffs and pitchforks. In its resemblance to such old tools of common folk, it is an appropriate item in the folk witch's collection.

Still, the modern stang truly rose to popularity among witches at the recommendation of Robert Cochrane (2016), a brilliant English witch interested in hereditary and folkloric forms of witchcraft and how they might be translated into modern practice. In the late 50's and 60's, Cochrane, who identified as a witch outside of the Wicca movement headed by Gardner, recommended the use of the forked staff or stang as a kind of combined tool: a staff used in all the ways a staff may be used, but also an altar representing the horned figure of the witch's teacher or Devil of the craft. The stang continues its popularity today among contemporary witches for its beauty, its simplicity, and the elegance of its appearance when decorated with a chain of daisies or topped with an animal skull.

Even simpler yet, we see the efficiency and functionality of the twig bundle or primitive whisk in the folk witch's repertoire. Being smaller than the broom or stang, the whisk cannot bear weight during a spirit flight session, but like the end of a broom, it can be rhythmically beat against the floor or the palm of the other hand, resulting in a repetitive percussion that resembles hoofbeats in dried grass, a helpful rhythm to facilitate the trance state and engage the otherworldly senses necessary for successful spirit flight. Unlike the staff or broom, the witch's whisk is compact and portable, making it a worthy alternative for small spaces and traveling craft. The whisk is reminiscent of the bundle of twigs said in our lore to be toted by Cain, elsewhere identified as the Man in the Moon, one of the earliest sorcerers in our art (Whitehouse, 2016). It is also reminiscent of the Devil's club or bundle of thorns described as a part of early colonial witches' sabbats (Davis, 1975).

However the modern witch chooses to implement the broom, staff, or stang in flight work, he can rest assured that such tools are time-tested and rooted thoroughly in the lore of our ancestors. Such objects carry with them a kind of charm of accrual; their use over many centuries imbues them with qualities conducive to our work, connected to our legacy, and evocative of the hundreds of years of workings of witches past.

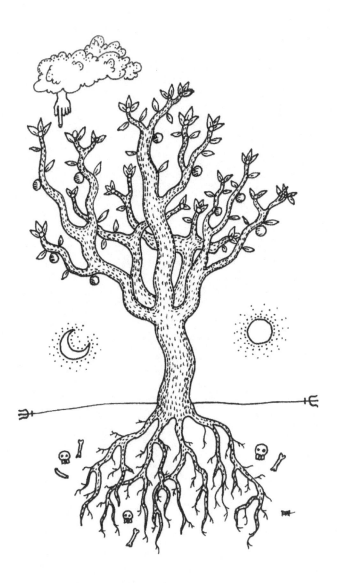

Via Arborum

In the countryside, dry leaves whistle on the cool evening breeze. It is late in the autumn. October has cooled the wind and drawn color from the boughs of ancient trees, their roots gnarling and twisting about the rock and bone beneath them.

The witch walks slowly and intentionally in the waning light, approaching his chosen ritual spot on the small farm: a single elder tree. Earlier this year, its flowers clustered like pale stars, smelling sweet like honey and cream, then fallen, each star dropped to the ground below, giving way to fat, plump berries. But all of that is over. The elder tree prepares itself now for winter and for stasis, standing on the precipice of life and death. A gate-keeper. One the witch means to approach this night for its powerful aid.

He sits before the elder tree, focusing on his witch-sight, on calling his senses of the otherworld so as to be able to perceive her more clearly for what she truly is: an ancient being, a teacher, an ancestor. He speaks the old charm associated with the elder spirit:

> *Mother, give me some of thee,*
> *and when I am become a tree,*
> *I shall give thee some of me.*[*]
> *For I am of thee, and thou art mine,*
> *and I have nothing which is not thine.*

With these words, the warlock pours some of the water he brought along as an offering. It gurgles at the roots of the tree, then seeps quickly into the soil, a gift accepted. He takes one leaf from a branch of the tree—no more. He knows that, in our lore, the Elder Mother is quick to anger by the slightest offense, sending curse and plague upon mortals fool enough to take more than is offered. She must be approached kindly, respectfully, and with the greatest of care.

At the base of the old tree, where the roots pull away from the soil, the witch spies an opening—just a small hole—one perfect to consecrate as a portal to the otherworld. He holds the elder leaf offered in his hand: a gifted talisman to aid the journey to come.

> *Here do I speak a sain of going.*
> *Sain of seven paters, one.*
> *Sain of seven paters, two.*
> *Sain of seven paters, three.*
> *Sain of seven paters, four.*

---

[*] This charm is difficult to date, but is most likely early modern in origin. The concept of the "Elder Mother" as a spiritual being is likely far older. The charm is noted in Henderson's 1886 edition of *Notes on the Folk-lore of the Northern Counties of England* and many other similar texts of the mid-1800s.

Sain of seven paters, five.
Sain of seven paters, six.
*Sain of seven paters, seven.**

He takes a deep breath, feeling his spirit loosen from his form of bone and flesh. That dark passage where the roots lift from the soil—that has become a door, one he will take to the otherworld to conduct his workings on this eve. As he approaches the passage, he can sense the roots of the tree beneath the grass, its form like lightning, ever-reaching, tangled in the roots of other plants and trees, wound up in the bones and remains of decaying animals, in minerals, the bones of the earth. The tree is connected to every other living thing. It reaches and thirsts and breathes. Those lines become tunneling hallways mirroring the structure of the tree's branches, each one leading to a door, to another point of entry. Each door bears a unique sign upon it that is difficult to discern. The witch must focus his sight in order to perceive the lines and carvings upon each one. He knows that each door will lead to a different lesson, to a different journey. He must choose.

~ 👉 ~

Trees have always possessed a unique fascination for witches in our old lore. Leland

---

* One of many "sain" charms that employs the counting motif traditional in Scottish folk craft. This version is adapted from Carmichael's (1900) *Carmina Gadelica.*

(1892), who is sometimes called the grandfather of contemporary witchcraft, wrote of the importance of the walnut tree to Italian witches, who in the lore are said to flock there by spirit flight to attend revelries and ritual to honor the father and teacher of witches. In the ritual example narrated above, we see the significance of the elder tree, which has been described in our lore as a favorite of witches around the world (Roud & Simpson, 2000). The rowan tree, which has been favored in folk magic for its powers against curses and malevolent fae—often including witches—was incorporated into the use of cunning craft practitioners across the British Isles. As modern practitioners who now understand that the cunning folk preserved much of our tradition for the ages, we can view this body of superstition as somewhat ironic, making the rowan tree useful in both the work of witchcraft itself and against malevolent witches who would turn their craft against neighbors.

On a grander scale, the symbolism of the tree offers us, as modern witches, an important gate into the workings of the spirit and our ongoing lessons in the otherworld. The language of animism often translates the structure of the universe into a living tree with branches representing paths between worlds. We see this symbol present in the pre-Christian Norse lore surrounding Yggdrasil, which holds the nine worlds together in Germanic myth:

An ash I know there stands,
Yggdrasil is its name,
A tall tree, showered
With shining loam.
From there come the dews
That drop in the valleys.
It stands forever green
Over Urd's well. (*The Poetic Edda*, 1969)

At Yggdrasil's base sit the three Norns, the keepers of human fates, and their three wells: each at the end of a single root that falls into a distinct world.

More influential still is the lingering presence of the Assyrian Moon Tree, which still shapes esotericism today. While many magical practitioners think of the Qabalistic Tree of Life as the central motif for understanding spiritual cosmologies, it is actually predated by and modeled after its ancestor and original, the Assyrian Tree of Life, a glyph of interdependence that scholars have noted to have distinct pagan origins, later adapted and incorporated into Abrahamic mysticism (Parpola, 1993). Even thousands of years in the past, sorcerers looked to the tree as an ancient symbol of our connection to the universe around us.

In fact, Frazier (1922) discusses the powerful role trees would have played as the first gods of our ancestors. Their massive height and ability to provide homes to smaller life forms would have impressed the ancients who lived among the forest. Their longevity and power to reproduce themselves would have identified them as potent spiritual allies. Their ability to provide food in the form of fruit and nuts would have cemented their role as generous Old Ones, providers of nourishment, shelter, and life.

What's more, we see in the image of these ancient trees the power to reach between worlds. Their branching structure above the soil, reaching for the sun, is a mirror image of their root structure below the soil, to the land of the dead and of the fae. Trees spread in both directions: into the dark and the light, into the waking and dreaming worlds, and when winter comes and the sun is blotted out and the ground sealed with ice, the tree is safe, retreating its vital energy into that world below our world, into the dark and mysterious chthonic realms that we witches are uniquely empowered to venture by our craft. In this way, trees themselves are Old Ones. The spirits of Oak, Ash, and Thorn have long been our mentors and guides. In learning from these and other ancient tree spirits, we gain the power to pass those forbidden boundaries.

One of the concepts that often confounds new witches is the relationship between spirit and form. As modern animists, folk witches hold that every living thing possesses a spirit, yet that spirit may present itself in any number of ways, both as a representative of that living thing itself and as a sort of emanation of a larger spirit that animates all individual creatures that are a part of its existence. For example, when we speak of the spirit of the apple tree, we might be speaking of the spirit of an individual apple tree, but we might also be speaking of the Apple Tree spirit, one being that presents itself in the form of millions of apple trees around the world. Both perspectives are valid and very real, but in the work of spirit flight, it is more common to encounter the ruling spirit who governs multitudes under its name. In this way, the spirit is present in the living form (the body), but is also larger than its individual components. The spirit is the keeper of the blueprint of its nature, the guardian of the living pattern that makes up its cycles and behaviors, the key to its very essence. It is this spirit that offers us grander lessons in the art magical since it reduces and concentrates, as if by alchemical art, all of the keys and lessons that make up what "apple tree" truly is.

In fact, the tree spirits were so influential that they were preserved in Celtic lore and cemented in connection with the alphabet we now know as ogham. In the *Auricept na nEces,* written in the 7th century, the origins of the ogham are described:

What are the place, time, person, and cause of the

> invention of the Ogham? Not hard. Its place the
> island of Ireland where the Irish live. In the time of
> Bres, son of Elatha, king of Ireland it was invented.
> Its person Ogma, son of Delbaeth, brother to Bres,
> for Bres, Ogma, and Delbaeth are the three sons of
> Elatha, son of Delbaeth there. Now Ogma, one
> well-skilled in speech and in poetry, invented the
> Ogham. The cause of its invention, as proof of his
> ingenuity, and that this speech should belong to the
> learned...

This passage connects the alphabet to the Celtic god Ogma, who had the power to bind men to his will with his speech, but the connection to the tree spirits is provided in another text. The "tree ogham" is but one form of ogham among many. Its letters have been associated in medieval texts with bodies of water, birds, dogs, parts of the hand, and much more. It is an alphabet of hidden meanings and a flexible system of cipher that can be applied in an endless multitude of ways, but modern ogham practitioners like myself find the tree ogham particularly useful for its ability to draw on the vast body of lore associated with individual tree spirits, imbuing each letter with potent energy for spirit work. The *Buile Shuibi*, written sometime in the 1100s, provides clues as to these spirits:

> Thou oak, bushy, leafy,
> thou high beyond all trees;
> o hazlet, little branching one,
> o fragrance of hazel-nuts.

O alder, thou art not hostile,
delightful is thy hue,
thou art not rending and prickling
in the gap wherein thou art.

O little blackthorn, little thorny one;
o little black sloe tree;
o water cress, little green-topped one,
from the edge of spring.

O minnen of the pathways,
thou art sweet beyond herbs,
o little green one, very green one,
o herb on which grows the strawberry.

O apple tree, little apple tree,
much art thou shaken;
o quicken, little berried one,
delightful is thy bloom.

O briar, little arched one,
Thou grantest no fair terms,
thou ceasest not to tear me
till thou hast thy fill of blood.

O yew tree, little yew tree,
in churchyards thou art conspicuous;
o ivy, little ivy,
thou art familiar in the dusky wood.

O holly, little sheltering one,
thou door against the wind;
o ash tree, thou baleful one,
hand weapon of the arrior.

O birch, smooth and blessed,
thou melodious, proud one,
delightful each entwining branch
in the top of thy crown.

These lines are echoed by other medieval texts of the era that emphasize the personalities and properties of tree spirits as sheltering, generous, mischievous, aggressive, or intellectual, their individual natures forming a palette of symbol conducive to magical work and very naturally aligned with the ogham letters outlined in the table provided.

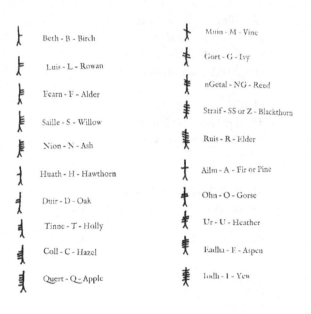

Beth - B - Birch

Luis - L - Rowan

Fearn - F - Alder

Saille - S - Willow

Nion - N - Ash

Huath - H - Hawthorn

Duir - D - Oak

Tinne - T - Holly

Coll - C - Hazel

Quert - Q - Apple

Muin - M - Vine

Gort - G - Ivy

nGetal - NG - Reed

Straif - SS or Z - Blackthorn

Ruis - R - Elder

Ailm - A - Fir or Pine

Ohn - O - Gorse

Ur - U - Heather

Eadha - E - Aspen

Iodh - I - Yew

Together, these letters form sounds that articulate easily into incantatory strings, sigil work, and talismanic creations as an aid to spirit flight and to connect with the ruling spirits of the trees with which they correspond.

Evidence of spirit flight work associated with the ogham is present in the 1300s text of the *In Lebor Ogaim* (The Book of Oghams). In this text, we find the first illustration of the journeying sigil that has been called "Fionn's Window" or "Fionn's Ridgepole."

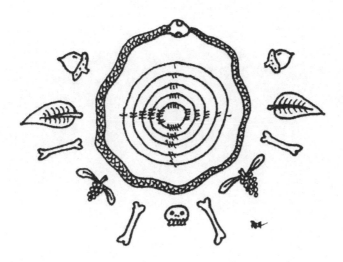

The concentric circles upon which the ogham are struck depict the rings around the central pole used to hold up a medieval home in the region, a hole through which smoke from the hearth could pass into the sky—and a natural vehicle for the spirit flight performed by Irish and Scottish folk-magical practitioners of the era. This sigil remains today a useful visual tool for those who perform spirit flight work with the aid of or in order to connect with tree spirits.

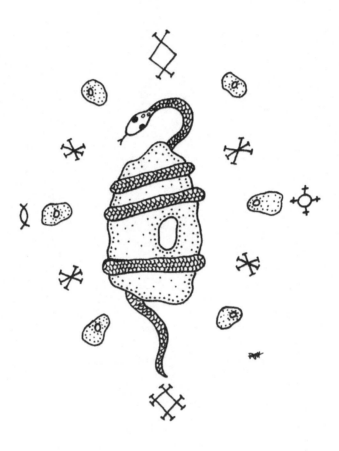

Via Lapidum

With the holed stone in hand, the witch proceeds to her attic working space, climbing the stairs, drawing the curtains closed, and lighting a single candle upon the bare table in the center of the room. They set the hagstone before the candle, arranging a collection of gathered treasures from walks taken through the land during the last year: dried and pressed deadnettle flowers, acorns gathered from an old and twisted oak, and snail shells bleached in the sun. In the center of this assemblage, the hagstone gazes with its eye of rock, a tunnel to the otherworld, a talisman holding within it the keys to the secret of caverns beneath the surface of the earth.

Having assembled the altar for the working, the witch draws a deep breath. Here are the totems of the spirits of the land, of flora and of fauna, of flesh and of leaf. Here are the footsteps of the Old Ones, ingrained and incarnate in the matter of this earth, each of them once vibrant with the energy of a life now passed into shadow. The residual vibrance lingers there, the witch knows, pulsing beneath the surface, like an echo of a story told in *another room, down a hall one cannot see.*

The words are a mingling of old craft, saved from the ravages of time in tattered fragments. Preserved here are the songs of the witch's ancestors and the words of the old lore, recalling the path of the serpent, the ancient use of caves in the old craft, the old name of Puca as the black and white goat of the sabbat—another name for the Devil of our craft—the ancient teacher who lies at the end of that tunneling passage the witch now seeks. The witch now begins the charm to conjure the holed stone thrice* and bless it as a gate to the Old Ones:

> *I conjure you, O adder stone*
> *tunneled by the serpent's body.*
>
> *I conjure you, O hag stone,*
> *bore through even as the caves of the earth*
> *and the rushing streams upon it.*
>
> *I conjure you, O holey stone,*
> *through which the Old Ones pass.*
>
> *Hal, hal, aoirinn,*
> *hiu bhidil hiu bhi*
> *hal, hal, aoirinn,*
> *Puca Geal, Puca Dubh.†*

---

* An alternative charm for conjuring the holed stone, which involves an appeal to the goddess Diana, is provided in Leland's (1899) *Aradia: Gospel of the Witches of Italy.*

† The Gaelic charm here is adapted from Carmichael's (1900) *Carmina Gadelica.* "Puca Geal, Puca Dubh" is the author's own deviation from the

The witch now focuses on feeling the stone with their hand: its nooks and crags, its smooth, rounded edges, its coolness, the concaved well in the center that becomes the hole bore through it by countless centuries of water. The center begins to feel almost soft, as if one could push through it. Slowly at first, the witch pushes. The cool of the stone's surface gives way and enlarges in the witch's spirit vision, becoming the cold stone walls of a great cavern. At their feet flows the stream that has bore through the rock for centuries, its water bright and luminous.

Following the stream into the interior of the cave, all other light gives way to velvet dark. Ahead, the witch perceives what looks like the light of a small fire around the next curve of the cave. They know that this is the place of spiritual gathering: the location of the hidden meeting among the spirits and the people. Here is where lessons will be offered, where wisdom will be shared, where spirits will be nourished...

~ ☞ ~

The lore of the holed stone and its relationship with witchcraft is heavy with antiquity. Whether termed hag stone, serpent stone, adder stone, Odin-stone, or witch-stone, the simple stone found near water with a self-bored hole has

---

formula, here referring to the Old One known as Puca in forms both white and black.

been the subject of numerous charms. Pliny's description of the adder stone connects it thoroughly with the serpent, an emblem of the witch's teacher and master of our craft:

> It was long held that at the season when adders slough, many meet in one place, rarely seen by man, when the largest casts its skin in the form of a perfect tube, through which the others quickly wriggle, each one leaving a coat of slime on it. This, in drying, assumes a globular shape with a hole in the centre, and thus was formed the druidical bead of the old antiquaries; the adder stone of the vulgar... (Duns, 1896)

It is not inaccurate to say that, in the witch's passage through the holed stone by way of charm and spirit flight, the witch embodies the lore of the serpent, winding and coiling into the cold and dark depths of the earth to seek the otherworld's passage.

Ironically, we see the hagstone used in our lore to deter a witch's efforts at riding or tormenting the victim in spirit form. Timbs (1873) describes this tradition of magical defense:

> A stone with a hole in it, suspended at the head of the bed, would effectually stop the nightmare; hence it was called a hagstone, as it prevents the troublesome witches from sitting upon the sleeper's stomach. The same amulet is tied to the key of a stable door to deter witches from riding horses over the country.

If we approach the holed stone as charmed vehicle rather than mere talisman, the connection here becomes clearer. As an icon of the serpent's winding path and the boring of water through the earth, the holed stone can both offer passage to the otherworld and deter magical intruders by redirecting them to another location via the stone's transvective properties.

The holed stone, then, is a simulacrum of the magic of caves and of serpents and running water in their ability to pass into hidden depths. In modern craft usage, it is a simple, portable object used to conjure those potencies in the art of spirit flight, a tool providing a chthonic gateway that is, at the same time, contagious of the serpent's magic.

But the connection of the holed stone with the serpent goes further than mere tunnel-boring. In its ability to shed skin and renew itself, the serpent is imbued with the magic of rebirth, the ability to leave one's old self behind and emerge as something renewed and invigorated. This reflexive self-emergence is evident in our art of flight; while the stone itself serves as doorway and vehicle, it is through the gate of the self that witches pass in our work, emerging in a new and more potent spirit form so that we may pass into the otherworld as one of its own, as something that is both the self and something other and more than the self. It is the ancient symbol of the ouroboros, the serpent devouring itself to form a circle or ring. It is Jormungandr, the serpent whose body encloses the world that is known.

Leland (1892) notes an interesting mythological connection with the holed stone: Odin, the most sorcerous of the Norse gods, was said to have transformed himself into a worm in order to pass through a hole in a rock and steal the mead of poetry, yielding another once-common name for the holed stone: the Odin stone. He further connects the holed stone with the gifts of magical sight and perception:

> ...the English saying, "He can see through a mill-stone as far as any man" really had its origin in the belief that by looking through the hole in a mill-stone the sight was improved. As every mill-stone has a hole through it there is not much sense in the literal acceptation of the proverb. But if looking through the hole improved the sight, then he whose sight was most improved would see furthest.

Although Leland does not go so far as to make the connection between the holed stone and spirit flight practices, the relationship here is clear. If one can look through a window in order to perceive the forms of the otherworld, one can also climb through it via magical operation, following the mythic example of Odin.

Interestingly, the Scottish lore of the adder

stone emphasizes its curative properties. We can understand this connection best by viewing the self-holed stone as simulacrum of the serpent's process of self-renewal as in Pliny's description. In its aspect as an animist spirituality, folk witchcraft allows us to reach into the otherworld to procure charms and spiritual knowledge, and magically speaking, it makes sense to deduce that the gate-as-talisman can be charmed to release curative magics directly into a vessel of water, which can then be used:

> A flat whorl of hard sandstone, which belonged to the famous witch called Meg Elson, who lived in the Fingaul district of Kirkmaiden, Wigtownshire, about the beginning of this century. It was used for curing elf-shot. A red woolen thread was put through the hole, and it was dipped three times in water taken from a well on which the sun did not shine by a girl with red or yellow hair. A rhyme, in what was supposed to be Gaelic, was said over the water, which was then given to the cow to drink. (Black, 1894)

We see the importance of water to this charm; as the water is drawn from the well, so too is power drawn through the hole in the adder stone from its source in the otherworld to imbue the water with its potency.

For witches seeking to procure their own holed stone for magical usage, my recommendation is to venture to a creek with fast-running water. Take with you a toothpick or a needle. Often, the hole formed in a stone by running water is small and plugged with dirt or silt, making it easy to overlook these valuable objects and mistake them for stones with mere dents or blemishes. The only way to know for sure whether the hole goes through the stone entirely is to test it with a toothpick or needle, prodding gently, then submerging the stone in water to wash away the blockage.

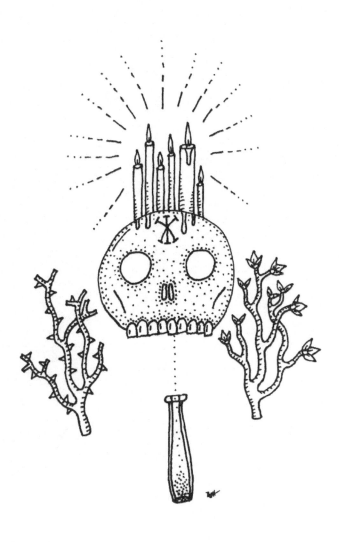

Via Mortuorum

On a midnight during the waning moon, the witch prepares her working space for the charm. First come the ornaments of flora and fauna: the body of a moth gifted on the porch in August, the shed skin of a praying mantis, dried leaves and acorns from an old oak tree, and the skull of a goat that died on a farm. These relics of the land are laid upon the altar carefully, arranged intuitively in a manner conducive to the work. Here are the signs of the spirits of the land. They will lend power and grace to the working to come. Then, the central candle is lit along with a prayer spoken into the dark:

> *Here I set a fire bright*
> *with Brigid and Mary in its light,*
> *upon the ceiling and the floor,*
> *on every wall and every door.* *

The match crackles loudly as it is struck. The flame of the

---

* Brigid and Mary are both traditionally invoked in Scottish folk charms. The kindling charm here is again adapted from the *Carmina Gadelica*.

candle dances, casting shadows about the room. The working space has been sanctified.

The witch removes a small bottle from her shelf of stored ingredients. Its glass is blurred and opaque with age, but gazing into the bottle, the witch can still make out bits of root and rock among its contents: an ounce of graveyard dirt, procured with love and offering from an old cemetery down the road, its soil made rich with ancestors, its grounds hallowed by the old trees that cast their shade upon the now illegible headstones. Closing her eyes, the witch remembers the bread she left as an offering to the dead there, the solemn request she spoke before taking the soil, the cool, consenting breeze that passed through the trees.

In her dominant hand, the witch holds up high the bottle of soil over the black candle in an authoritative gesture. With her other hand, she lights the dried bundle of mugwort. Its perfume is dense and sour. She weaves the bundle about the air, casting its smoke about the altar space, around the bottle of graveyard dirt she holds aloft. She is awakening the power within it, stirring the bit of spirit essence that lies dormant there, calling it forth:

Honored ones, from your graves, I call you.
With prayer and fumigation, I call you.
With bone and leaf, I call you.
With love and offering, I call you.

Teh Beh Ripahr
Ichi Pass
Ez Peh Lah Tem

Ex Wah Yameh
Queh Warren
*Peh Riesh Teh**

Come, Come, Come.

The last two lines of the charm become a chant, building in intensity and speed as the witch fans the mugwort smoke about the air: "Peh Riesh Teh, Come, Come, Come!"

Suddenly, she falls silent. She feels several small shadows in the corners of the room, on the very edge of her perception. The dead have come.

> *Open now the passage for me*
> *that I might visit the realm of the dead*
> *and pass safely to and from that kingdom.*

The mugwort smoke has done its work: she feels her consciousness loosened enough to perceive what will become her entrance to the otherworld. Thrice she knocks upon the floor. Slowly, with eyes closed, holding great focus and intent. At the first knock, she hears the depth of its echo, as if there is no ground beneath the floor, but instead, a large, hollow passage. At the second knock, she perceives with her witch-sight the percussion, the resonance within her bones. At the third knock, she is at last able to perceive the door. What was once mere floor is now a gate waiting to be

---

* A phonetic rendering of a necromantic charm recorded in the 16th century manuscript titled *The Book of Magic*, Folger Shakespeare Library MS. V.b.26.

opened so that her spirit might slip through. With a slow breath, she moves her spirit to open the door, allowing her body to fall deep into the trance that will last until she returns safely from the journey.

~ 🖎 ~

Necromancy, the magical art of communicating with the dead, has long been associated with witchcraft, and for good reason. One of our oldest scraps of lore is from the bible itself; the Witch of Endor, yielding to the request of Saul, conjures the dead Samuel to speak with him by her art. It is worth noting here that, in this story, Saul has banished all witches and sorcerers from Israel. While the Witch of Endor agrees to Saul's request, what she offers gives no comfort or guidance. The spirit of Samuel predicts Saul's death, and the witch insists on feeding the horrified Saul before he leaves in a supposed act of comfort. We can only guess what manner of charm she might have used upon the food of the king who banished her and her people only to command her assistance at his beck and call. We can read the Witch of Endor as a sly figure who uses necromancy to offer her oppressor nothing but suffering in his moment of need—and not unjustly.

The *Greek Magical Papyri* record the use of specific charms and incantations to conjure the spirits of the dead in ancient times. Often, necromantic charms from this period involve calls to Hekat or Hecate (who is also known as a Queen of Witches in her own right) in her aspect as ruler of the shades of the dead and the underworld. We even see in Scot's (1584) work a reference to a necromantic rite:

> By the mysteries of the deep, by the flames of Banal, by the power of the East, and by the silence of the night, by the holy rites of Hecate, I conjure and exorcise thee thou distressed spirit, to present thyself here, and reveal unto me the cause of thy calamity, why thou didst offer violence to thy own liege life, where thou art now being, and where thou wilt hereafter be.

Here, we see echoes of the most ancient necromancers of legend. One thinks of the mythic sorceress Circe instructing Odysseus on the rites necessary to commune with the spirit of Tiresius in the depths of Hades.

In its most basic nature, though, the opening of gates between the living and the dead need not be a fearful event. The spirits of those who have gone before understand what it is to be human because they have lived the human experience themselves. Their ability to empathize with us is great, though their perspective is made broad by their passage into the otherworld. While witches pass into the otherworld frequently for short intervals, the dead have traveled there permanently, their consciousness shifted into a new nature, an entirely different way of perceiving and existing. Even images and experiences that living persons might identify as horrific are not necessarily intended as harmful; we must remember and ever seek to understand that the spirits of the dead were once as we are, but no longer. Their nature, their presence, and their means of communicating with us are now different. Not evil, but merely *different*. Green (1899) describes well how the veneration of the dead evolved into the surviving animistic practices known as the faery faith:

> The Second Stone Age men, it is said, cremated their dead who were worthy of reverence, and worshipped their shades, and the nursery tales of pixies and goblins and elves are but the mythical remains of their once prevailing religion—universal the world over. The inception of this ancestral worship probably took place during that period known as the Neolithic Age, when the moon, stars, and sun no longer remained the mysterious in life to be feared and worshipped. In the dreary process of evolution a gradual development took place, and nature worship and ancestral veneration evolved into the more comprehensive systems of Buddha, Confucius, and the later polytheism of Greece, Ancient Tuscany, and Rome, leaving high and dry, stranded, as it were, in Northern Europe, Ireland, and North Britain, an undisturbed residuum of ante-chronological man's superstitions.

Despite Green's misuse of the term *evolution*, which smacks of his tone of superiority, the relationship he highlights between the spirits of the dead and the spirits of the land (and even the early beginnings of the great spirits we know as gods or Old Ones) is useful for understanding the fabric of folk craft itself. Our otherworld is murky, and the spirits of the dead cannot easily be separated from the spirits of the land and the Old Ones themselves.

This is not to suggest that passage into the realms of the dead is without its dangers. Far from it, our lore is ripe with tales of malevolent spirits who seek to cause suffering beyond the grave. The famous Demon of Glenluce was said to be the ghost of a man named Alexander Agnew, who had threatened Gilbert Campbell's family before his death for being denied aid in his poverty. After his death, Gilbert was prevented from achieving any success in his trade as a weaver by destructive poltergeist activity:

> ...Gilbert was oftentimes hindered in the exercise of his calling, or his working instruments (he being a weaver) being some of them broken, some cut, and yet could not know by what means his hurt was done. This continued till about the middle of November; when the devil came with new and extraordinary assaults, by throwing stones in at the doors and windows, and down the chimney, in great quantities,

> and with great force... (*The History of Witches, Ghosts, and Highland Seers*, 1800)

Upon the involvement of a local priest, the torment upon the family only increased:

> ...the persons within the family suffered many losses, as the cutting of clothes, the throwing of peat, the pulling down of turf and seal from the roof and walls of the house, the stealing of their apparel, and the pricking of their flesh and skin with pins.

Eventually, the spirit speaks to the Campbell family from beneath a bed in a most frightening manner, describing itself as connected with the workings of witches in Glenluce. While it is impossible to hazard a guess as to the validity or logic of this tale, it is worth wondering whether the spirit of Alexander Agnew was more than a mere ghost, but an entity descended from or working with other powerful beings in the area.

In fact, the connection between witches and the spirits of the dead is a strong one across the world; the Romanian spirits known as *strigoi* (from which a variety of vampiric and ghoulish lore originates) are often associated with the spirits of living or deceased witches. The word *strigoi* itself is etymologically bound to the word *striga*, meaning *witch* or *wizard* (Du Nay, 1977).

The only remote equivalent of these spirits in the British Isles are the fae or Good People.

Though described in modern children's stories as small and cherubic, the Good People of the old lore are very diverse, and often dangerous. From these beings come the tales of the redcap, who dyes his hat red in the blood of his victims, the bean-sidhe, who appears as a dark phantom wailing to foretell death, and the kelpie, a horse that lures its victims into climbing its back before diving into water to drown the fools. These denizens of the otherworld are frequently perceived near prehistoric burial mounds that are described in early modern lore as "fairy hills," emphasizing again the connection between otherworldly spirits and the realms of the dead. Evans-Wentz (1911) groups ghosts, demons, and fairies together as celebrants on All Hallows' Eve:

> All of this matter is definitely enough in line with the living Fairy-Faith: there is the same belief expressed as now about November Eve being the time of all times when ghosts, demons, spirits, and fairies are free, and when fairies take mortals and marry them to fairy women; also the beliefs that fairies are living in secret places in hills, in caverns, or underground—palaces full of treasure and open only on November Eve. In so far as the real fairies, the Sidhe, are concerned, they appear as rulers of the Feast of the Dead or Samain, as the controllers of all spirits who are then at large...

None of this is intended to frighten curious young necromancers from proceeding with the workings of this particular gateway of spirit flight. The intention here is merely to offer this fair warning: proceed with care and respect. Too often, we the living imagine ourselves immortal. We forget that one day, our bones will also lie within the earth, our forms returned to soil. As they are, so shall we be in time. We must treat the spirits of the dead as honored beings worthy of respect, and we must certainly keep our wits about us while proceeding with craft that concerns their realm.

In the charm described in the narrative section at the beginning of this chapter, the witch makes use of graveyard dirt. While the grimoires circulating in Europe in the medieval and early modern periods more commonly called for actual body parts procured from corpses in their necromantic formulas, this is unsavory to modern practitioners for a variety of reasons, and graveyard dirt is a perfectly potent substitute. It contains actual matter from the dead mingling with the molecules in the soil, and it connects us with the dirt beneath our feet as a threshold between the living and the dead.

While many modern practitioners think of graveyard dirt as belonging solely to hoodoo and other forms of folk magic in the Southern United States, its use as a potent magical ingredient actually transcends multiple folk-magical traditions; in fact, we see a reference to the use of soil taken from a grave in the famous *Grimorium*

Verum, written sometime in the mid-1700s. In this charm, the practitioner is instructed to attend a midnight mass, and after offering an incantation, must go immediately to the cemetery and stop at the first grave to which she is drawn:

> ...take a fistful of earth and scatter it as you would scatter grain in a field, saying in a low voice:
>
> 'He who is in dust awakens from his tomb, and rises from his ashes and answers the questions that I will make of him...' (Peterson, 2007)

The ritual of knocking upon the ground to call the spirits of the dead is an old one, described in Andrew Lang's 1893 introduction to Kirk's (1691) *The Secret Commonwealth of Elves, Fauns, and Fairies: A Study in Folklore and Psychical Research*:

> In many ways, as when persons carried off to Fairyland meet relations or friends lately deceased, who warn them, as Persephone and Steenie Steenson were warned, to eat no food in this place, Fairyland is clearly a memory of pre-Christian Hades. There are other elements in the complex mass of Fairy tradition, but Chaucer knew "the Fairy Queen Proserpina," as Campion calls her, and it is plain that in very fact, "the dread Persephone," the "Queen over death and the dead," had dwindled into the lady who borrows Tamlane in the ballad. Indeed Kirk mentions but does not approve of this explanation, "that those subterranean people are departed souls." Now, as was said, the dead are

> dwellers under earth. The worshippers of Chthonian Demeter (Achaia) beat the earth with wands; so does the Zulu sorcerer when he appeals to the Ancestors. And a Macdonald in Moidart, being pressed for his rent, beat the earth, and cried aloud to his dead chief, "Simon, hear me; you were always good to me."

Unlike the ceremonial magicians of the medieval period who performed necromancy to enslave and master the spirits of the dead, the folk witch calls to the dead in kinship and love. This is not strictly an ethical point of view, but also a practical one; approach a spirit on respectful and friendly terms, and they are more likely to agree to your request (not unlike when asking a favor from any living person). This is why it is necessary to bring a suitable offering before taking soil or anything else from a graveyard. Good manners go a long way in the otherworld.

In voyaging to the land of the dead, which presents itself in the lore we have discussed as a subterritory of Elphame, the witch should have specific goals in mind: either communication with a person who has passed or a favor one hopes to implore from the denizens of that land. As always, any promises of offerings in exchange for favors granted should be honored with haste so as not to offend the spirits of the dead who have so kindly aided the witch's passage through their kingdom.

Via Veneficium

October has come at last, drying the leaves of oak and ash trees to paper, casting its chill upon the night air, lengthening the darker hours. These are nights for old charms, for gazing into shadow and spending the hard-won treasures of the summer months.

The witch clutches the small jar to his chest, feeling its potency. He has tended the spirits of this land well in their growing season. The pale moonflowers of the datura stramonium, the infamous thornapple of our lore, stretched open like white mouths in August. He watered them, tended them, waiting patiently for the growth to be complete. He shook the thorny, dried pod to collect seeds for next year's generation. In the tradition of witches gone before, he gathered their leaves, crushed them, and heated them in oil to render his liniment with beeswax, straining and pouring the golden-green treasure carefully into its jar.

Now is the time for the old charm, for the poisoner's charm, for the Devil's hour. Now is the time for shadow-flight and vision work in the otherworld. Gazing at the moon, the witch feels the pull of the old sabbat like *the pull of the tide on black waters. He is being called home to that other land, to the place where his teachers and brethren witches mingle and nourish themselves in spirit form.*

As he lights the candle before the deer skull and ivy laid on his altar, the witch calls to Old Scratch as the father and teacher of witches to bless his passage through the sabbat gate:

> *Old One, I seek after you this night.*
> *Bless me on the path to the hidden feast.*
> *Nema livee, morf su reviled tub*
> *noishaytpmet ootni ton suh deel sus*
> *tshaiga sapsert that yeth*
> *vigrawf eu za sesapsert rua*
> *suh vigrawf derb iliad rua yed sith*
> *suh vig neveh ni si za thre ni nud*
> *eeb liw eyth muck modgnik eyth*
> *main eyth eeb dwohlah nevah*
> *nit ra chioo, retharf rua.*[*]

He hears the wind beating against the sides of the house. With his powers of perception, he can feel a low echo from within the cavernous eyes of the deer skull, like a low voice calling from the depths of a distant cave.

The witch opens the jar of poisonous grease, yellow-green and opaque. He scoops a generous amount

---

[*] This incantation is, in fact, a backwards rendering of the Lord's Prayer, a witch's incantatory method described frequently in medieval and early modern lore.

onto two fingers, then proceeds to anoint himself, massaging the salve into his neck and chest, into his temples, into his wrists. A tune begins to come to him in the form of a low hum, growing until it becomes the old, familiar incantation:

> *Bazabi lacha bachabe*
> *Lamach cahi achabahe*
> > *Karrelyos*
> *Lamach Lamech Bachalyos*
> *Cabahagy Sabalyos*
> > *Baryolas*
> *Lagoz atha Cabyolas*
> *Samatha atha Famolas*
> > *Hurrahya*
> > *Hurrahya*
> > *Hurrahya*[*]

As he waits for the potency of the ointment to take hold, for its nightshade powers to invigorate his witch-sight and loosen his spirit, the witch chants the final lines of the charm, gazing into the eyes of the skull upon the altar. Slowly, the sensation builds—a warm tingling in his hands and feet, a slight feeling of inebriation, a loosening at his core like a tight knot coming slightly undone. With a long, noisome exhalation, the witch allows his spirit to slip from his own mouth, over his tongue and teeth, and into the

---

[*] While the infamous *Bazabi* chant achieved notoriety in Gerald Gardner's adaptations, its antiquity is authentic. Its first published appearance actually comes from Rutebeuf's 13th century *Le Miracle de Theophile*.

black void set before him: to careen and journey to that hidden gathering in the enclaves of the night.

~ 🖒 ~

The association of witches with the nightshade poisons has been infamous from ancient and medieval times, and this corner of our art has grown in popularity in recent years. Hatsis (2015) described how in 1487, Jean Vincent, a church inquisitor, proclaimed the use of these plants the work of dark sorcerers and witches:

> Poison witches...mix poisonous ingredients into love philters and ointments which disturb people's minds, transform their bodies, but usually serve only to kill the user. They claim to be transported far away, at night, to demonic Sabbats by the influence of these [same] drugs. The correct deduction, however, [is that] not one of these should be attributed to any natural power belonging to such drugs, but rather to the cunning of a demon...He [the demon] is the true operative cause, whereas these kinds of drugs are the secondary cause.

Ironically, as is often the case with medieval witch-lore, Vincent was not altogether wrong. While the chemical properties of the nightshades are real and their effects measurable, it is the influence of the plant's spirit that the witch feels most acutely when ritual, medicine, and dosage are properly understood and applied in modern practice.

Although work with nightshade plants and their spirits is rewarding and empowering for modern practitioners, there is so much misinformation regarding practices and dosages that this path possesses more dangers than other veins of our craft. For witches with underlying health conditions, I do not recommend nightshade work; instead, work with the artemisias mugwort and wormwood may be a suitable alternative, but speaking with one's doctor first is always recommended. Nor do I recommend any work with nightshades or artemisias for witches who have trouble following clear recipes and guidance or for those who cannot maintain basic safety measures in their daily lives. In short, if you are someone who cannot perform basic mathematics or who balks at the idea of helmets, seatbelts, or masks during a pandemic, nightshade work is not for you. It is easy to die when using poisonous plants such as these because these plants have evolved to draw us in with their siren-song, and discipline and restraint are the only things that can protect us when working the gate of poisons.

Some of our oldest historical references to nightshade craft pertain to the legendary mandrake, either mandragora officinarum, which has yellow flowers with elongated petals, or mandragora autumnalis, which boasts attractive purple flowers and slightly more rounded petals.

Dioscorides' (50 C.E.) ancient text *Materia Medica* describes the mandrake's effect as one that brings on a deep sleep and numbs the patient's sense of pain. It is mentioned in the Song of Solomon with the lines "The mandrakes give a smell. In our gates are all fruits: the new and the old, my beloved, I have kept for thee."

In fact, the 2nd century C.E. text *Physiologus* states that the mandragora and the Tree of Knowledge mentioned in Genesis are one and the same. This connection in ancient lore to me suggests that human beings, particularly those called to follow the wisdom-trail of the serpent, have maintained a symbiotic relationship with nightshade plants since the earliest years of civilization, that our fates are woven to such a degree that we are inextricably bound. This is perhaps not surprising on a literal level; tobacco, peppers, tomatoes, and potatoes all belong to the nightshade family as well.

The alkaloids responsible for the inebriating effects of mandrake, namely hyoscyamine and scopolamine, are also present in a number of other nightshades, including datura stramonium (also known as thornapple or jimsonweed), datura innoxia (moonflower), atropa belladonna (deadly nightshade), hyoscyamus niger (black henbane or stinking nightshade), and other less famous members of the Solanaceae family. These two alkaloids have been described as hallucinogens, but are more properly understood as deliriants. The visionary experiences they cause when used with reckless abandon are indistinguishable from ordinary reality, which is altogether different from recreational hallucinogens, the visual and auditory disturbances of which are easily differentiated from one's surroundings. An overdose of nightshades causes dangerous states of delirious excitability, to the extent that one might attempt to harm oneself or others out of sheer belief that what one experiences is real. This is the best-case scenario in the event of an overdose. Because these medicines interrupt the structures of the nervous system that control breathing and the beating of the heart, an overdose is most likely to end with a painful and terrifying death.

Yet, the old lore of the witches' ointment offers us a modern lesson in dosage and dilution, concepts that are all-important to nightshade work in modern craft. When an ointment prepared at a safe dilution is applied to the skin topically, its effects are mitigated by the body's natural barrier system. Only a small amount of the chemicals present in the plant are permitted to pass through. Oral dosages of tinctures and extracts were also used in previous ages before the demonization of these plants and the loss of specific preparation techniques to the general public.

Though I will not offer dosage

information here out of concern for the safety of readers who are ill-equipped to undertake this work, those who are ready to prepare nightshade medicine will find such information in Ratsch's (2005) *Encyclopedia of Psychoactive Plants* and Grieve's (1971) *A Modern Herbal*. The approach often used is to first identify via these texts the smallest possible dosage, then proceed to dilute it even further (with additional water or oil, depending on the preparation) to the point of surety that all harm can be avoided. For witches who have already proven capable of spirit flight without the aid of medicinal plants, the effects of their transvective work will be amplified a great deal, even with a well-diluted dosage in a very small amount. This is because, in herbal preparations, *more is not better.* A microdose of nightshade medicine is, in fact, more potent for the same reason that whiskey connoisseurs add a splash of water to their libations: at extreme potency, the art of the thing is actually lost. It is like trying to appreciate Satie's Gnossienne No. 1 by bending one's ear next to a blaring speaker. Too much amplification renders us deaf. The shrewd witch values the arts of dilution and dosage in order to best savor and appreciate the subtleties of nightshade medicine, which are actually more profound at lower dosages.

Even safer, gentler work (though still very much potent in its own right) can be done with the artemisias known as mugwort and wormwood. Both of these plants contain the chemical poison known as thujone, which is also famously present in the "drink of the green fairy" or absinthe. While many witches perform spiritual cleansing rituals sometimes called "smudging," using bundles of sage, folk and traditional witches often make use of mugwort instead. Its smoke is pungent, thick, and has a very mild psychoactive effect conducive to spirit work. Rather than expelling spiritual presences, I have noticed in my own practice that mugwort fumigation attracts helpful spirits, lending a balancing effect instead of a banishing effect. I think of this as the difference between the two: while a banishing effect is like taking an antibiotic, which strips the body of many forms of bacteria (both good and bad), a balancing effect is like a probiotic treatment. It calls in spiritual entities that balance out the effects of others, encouraging a spiritual ecosystem with balanced amounts of light and shadow. I have written before about the dangers of banishing. Do it once, and you'll be doing it forever. The spiritual world is not aseptic and sterile. It is diverse, interdependent, and complex. Utilizing mugwort fumigation in this way is less offensive to spirits and healthier for us as witches than scrubbing ourselves with the spiritual equivalent of bleach.

But let us return now to the Solanaceae. Discussions of nightshade work are too often dominated by talk of chemicals and alkaloids, as if witches working the gate of poison were merely escapists looking for their next high. Ratsch (2005) offers a useful differentiation between what we think of as "hallucinogenic" and "psychoactive"—

> In the modern Western world, the use of psychoactive plant products is very widespread, but their sacredness has been profaned. How many of us today, when we are sipping our morning coffee, are aware that the Sufis venerated the coffee bush as a plant of the gods and interpreted the stimulating effects of caffeine as a sign of God's favor? Who of us, lying in bed and smoking the first cigarette of the day, knows that tobacco is regarded as a gift of the gods that aids shamans in journeying into other realities? How many recall the frenzied Bacchanalia in honor of Dionysos as they drink a glass of wine with their lunch? And the evening beer in front of the television is drowned without any knowledge of the sacred origin of this barley drink.

Witches who partake in safe, diluted preparations of nightshade medicine looking to trip out will be disappointed; the effects of a safely diluted nightshade ointment or extract are more akin to having one or two alcoholic beverages or a brief inhalation of cannabis. (As a sidenote, the use of cannabis juice to anoint the forehead is mentioned in the 16th century manuscript called *The Book of Magic*, Folger Shakespeare Library MS. V.b.26., as a method for perceiving spirits.) More important than the mere physiological effects of plants are the spiritual ones, for by dressing ourselves with these plants, we drink deeply of their spiritual natures, sharing in their intoxicating magic.

Following the trail of our lore, we have already seen that the nightshade's powers are symbolized in the fruit of the Tree of Knowledge offered by the serpent in Eden: the folkloric beginning of humankind's journey of self-concept, intellect, and craft. The effects of the plant spirits of the nightshades are deeply bound to our ancestry as witches. I have often noticed in my practice that even incredibly small dosages of nightshade preparations are detectible to those with a penchant for witchcraft, whereas the unwise may feel very little or no effects whatsoever. It seems that witches, who dwell partly in this world and partly in the otherworld, have a fundamental acute sensitivity and appreciation for their magics in a way that others do not, a unique symbiosis with the spirits of poison.

Perhaps this is because witches are, in some ways, poisonous ourselves. Allow me to clarify. Like the nightshades, we do not seek to overthrow continents or leave a trail of ruin in our wake as modern witches, but something of our essence holds a careful darkness, a potency that arms us against the wickedness in the world around us. I have often said that poisonous plants are not nuclear plants. They aren't out to ruin us; they just don't want to be eaten, and those who cannot heed their warning will pay the price for their sin of ignorance. In magical tradition, almost all of the nightshade plants are identified as Saturnine in nature, being allied with the dead, the chthonic realms, and underworld workings. When we anoint ourselves with their medicine, we become Saturnine as well; we are dressed in the invisible, magical garments of poison itself, allowing us to reach with our roots beneath the surface of things, to perceive hidden currents, and to arrive at our otherworldly sabbat.

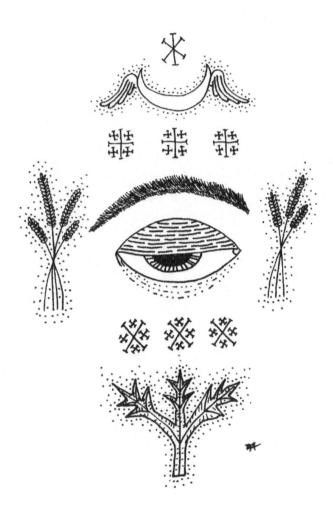

Via Somnium

The songs of crickets and frogs drift from the night outside through the open window. This day has been a long one, and night a welcome retreat. Collapsed from the exhaustion of housework and gardening under the heat of the sun, the witch walks across the house towards the comfort of their bed, bare feet against the cool floor.

From the bedside table, the witch takes up a small vial containing golden oil and applies a small amount to wrists, neck, and temples. This is an oil designed to assist in the dreaming art—lavender, catnip, and mugwort, steeped in warmed oil for a prolonged period of time, its fragrance rich and nutty with the plant essences imparted to its liquid.

Pulling back the blankets and sheets, the witch feels the pull of that needful sleep deeply—not only for the restoration of the body, but for the departure of the spirit for a time into that other realm, that place where wisdom and power can be restored when spent. With the tip of the thumb, the witch makes three crosses upon the spot where they will rest for the night, uttering the charm that will, *with the right intention, open the barrier to the dream-sabbat:*

> *In the days when the Old Ones walked,*
> *our queen's beloved lay cursed in his bed,*
> *and so she called in the moonlight*
> *to charm a place out of their dreaming.*
> *Three crosses on his bed she made*
> *to fix the gate to the sabbat-realm*
> *so that the unwise could not enter*
> *and no power of sleep or death*
> *could part them. So do I draw open*
> *the gates of the dreaming sabbat*
> *to dwell for a time in that fair land*[*].

Bending slightly over the bed, the witch blows gently. They feel their breath bend the barriers of the waking mind, hollowing out an entrance in the fabric of sheet and mattress, opening that invisible gate to the otherworld that will be used in dreams.

> *Old Ones, guard me on the path tonight*
> *that I might safely cross the threshold*
> *and return once more, by and by.*

~ 🖐 ~

---

[*] This charm is sourced in the lore presented in Leland's (1899) *Aradia: Gospel of the Witches of Italy*. Although Leland's version notes the lunar goddess as Tana, this myth is widespread, and the name elsewhere is provided as Selene.

As an animist magical tradition, folk witchcraft treats the consciousness of dream not as simple fantasy, but as an alternate mode of awareness that is valid in a way separate from waking reality. This is different in application, but similar in spirit to the importance of dreams in shamanism as described by Grim (1987):

> ...the individual Ojibway shaman's dream has both an immediate quality and a lasting impact. It often initiates the shamanic call and signifies the type of shamanic vocation. Although shamanic dreams vary greatly, there are recurring images and songs that are interpreted as a specific vocational call. This may be either to a lifelong shamanic role or to a temporary shamanic technique to meet a crisis situation.

Given the fact that Isobel Gowdie and many other witches of the early modern and medieval periods claimed to have experienced journeys to the spirit realm while sleeping in their beds, we would be wise to interpret their flights as callings or invitations to the otherworld. Because we have been taught to associate spirit flight, guiding spirits, talismans, folk magics, and basically all of animist spirituality with indigenous peoples outside of Europe, skeptics are quick to claim that Gowdie and others were merely delusional in their claims. White people, they would claim mistakenly, were too "evolved" beyond the practices of animism, even in the early modern age. We must resist this modern racist, ethnocentric urge and view our witch ancestors, instead, as practitioners of a folk tradition not unlike the shamans of the other cultures Europeans colonized and enslaved. They, too, experienced a call from the hidden realms. They, too, were brought before their Old Ones to learn hidden arts.

Scot (1584) observed the confusing and complex relationship between the witches' sabbat and the shifting landscapes of the dreaming mind. He writes:

> It is marvel that in dreams, witches of old acquaintance meet so just together, and conclude upon murders, and receive ointments, roots, powders, etc., (as witchmongers report they do, and as they make the witches confess) and yet lie at home fast asleep.

To confuse matters further, we must separate the old lore of witchcraft as preserved in texts like this one from the convenience of the dream-sabbat accusation from the perspectives of witch hunters at the time. On the one hand, it is simple enough to accuse someone of crimes in dream form when no physical proof is necessary to ensure a conviction. On the other hand, the history of the magical visionary experience has long attested the significance of dreams, and our own experiences as modern witches confirm the important role dreams play in magical practice. These experiences are real and impactful to practitioners.

In the ritual described in narrative form at the beginning of this chapter, we see a charm derived from Leland's (1895) *Aradia: Gospel of the Witches of Italy.* In this tale, Tana, a lunar Goddess, blesses the cursed Endymion so that they may visit and be together in his dreaming even though he lies in a state of perpetual sleep. This myth of the moon building a hidden dream realm out of magic is a potent one for modern witches. It is not incorrect to say that much of the violence and terror of the witch trials were driven by a fear not of outside intruders, but of ancestry and heritage. Many of those accused and killed practiced—or were merely suspected of practicing—simple folk charms with animistic origins. That anxiety, that tension that occurs from fearing and rejecting even the simplest, most basic aspects of one's own culture, has profound magical implications. Couple this fear with the misogyny rampant in those communities, and we arrive at the violent conclusion with which we are all unfortunately familiar.

With this perspective in mind, the phenomenon of the dream sabbat becomes clearer. The terrifying visions experienced by those whisked off to the sabbat are indicative of a kind of psychic buckling—a wound aggravated by blocking access to what is a natural experience for those with witchly inclinations. The moon has always been an emblem for witch ancestry— whether by association with Cain as first sorcerer, Hecate, Diana, or any number of other patron deities. In the myth of Endymion, we see a folkloric echo of the underlying symbolism of our dream-sabbat: how the Old Ones, in witnessing the self-rejection and self-loathing of our people, create a separate space accessed through the realm of dream under the guise of mere fantasy. They create a refuge, a haven, a hidden temple where those called to the art of witchcraft will always be welcomed, the door of the sabbat locked safely against any who do not bear the seed of craft within them.

Secret words and images shared in the dream-sabbat are a rich source of charms for the practitioner. Even words that do not seem to bear literal meaning often reveal themselves as charms through their connotations or their sound, which may be similar to the sound of names and words known to the practitioner. These utterances can be transcribed and their letters recombined to arrive at incantations useful in personal practice. Images, too, often suggest their meaning through connotation. These can be reduced to simple illustrations that function as talismans in one's craft. By drawing on the charms shared in the dream-sabbat regularly, witches can build a coterie of charms and art that are deeply connected to their ancestors, their familiars, and their personal needs and aesthetics.

The dark side of the dreaming arts presents the opportunity for witches to gain strength and overcome challenges—or to inflict horror upon the enemy. The word *nightmare* itself (though not related, as many presume, to the word *mare* for a female horse) refers to the Old English term *mare*: a demon, imp, or dark entity who causes suffering in the form of bad dreams.

Though many new witches assume that any negative experience in spirit flight is the result of demonic harrassment, this is rarely the case—in no small part because our Old Ones have been classified by the Judeo-Christian magical practitioners as demons themselves. Even the names of many goetic demons are derived from pagan Canaanite deities whose temples were destroyed and their peoples killed by the followers of the desert god Yahweh (or El, to use the oldest, Mesopotamian name for this entity). It is more useful for witches to view the challenger in the dream as a kind of test that may be passed by defeating it in a dedicated spirit flight session. This can be accomplished with the use of the fetch or the aid of one's familiars. The nightmare entity is often simply an energy that must be redirected—either made into an ally or absorbed so that its

power can be harnessed towards more productive
ends.

Via Aquum

The short glass jar in the witch's hand is heavy and cool, its contents sloshing about as he climbs down to his working place in the old root cellar. He has performed this ritual time and time again, and now it is needed once more. There are answers waiting at the sabbat. The wisdom of the Old Ones is needed again.

The witch sets to work, dragging the tip of the stang in a circle around the ritual space, a ring to focus the connective point where the two worlds will overlap, a circumference for the collision of world and otherworld.

Before me,
behind me,
on my right,
and on my left,
above me,
and below me,[*]

---

[*] Celtic charming traditions frequently refer to the directions about, above, and below the practitioner, establishing the charmer at the center of the spiritual universe.

and all throughout,
here do I set the ring about.

Moving slowly with intention, he lays a square linen cloth on the floor, upon which he arranges sacred artifacts to represent the King and Queen of Elphame, the mother and father of witches all, in their incarnations of flora and fauna: the shell of a snail, bones from a toad, fresh flowers cut from an apple bough. Using the old words to call the Lady and her Devil, he lights the central candle:

Commer, go ye before.
Commer, go ye.
If ye will not go before,
Commer, let me...[*]

When he feels the presence of the Old Ones in the room, he grows quiet, gathering up the jar of water to pour into a small cast iron pot:

Old Ones, grant me passage here
for I am of thee, and thou art mine,
and I have nothing which is not thine.

The pool within the pot is perfect black, still and reflective. The witch begins stirring the surface of the water gently with his finger in a counterclockwise direction

---

[*] This folk charm is associated with Nicneven and described as a conjuration in the infamous 1591 *Newes from Scotland*. "Commer" describes both one who arrives and a loved one, often a term for a woman.

(widdershins), allowing himself to fall into a gentle trance as the candle flickers.

> *Descendat spiritus*
> *in hoc speculum...* [*]

The witch stirs gently, barely touching the surface of the water, gazing into and behind the reflection of light upon it until it becomes deeper somehow, darker, less certain. Its black well becomes a tunnel in his witch-sight, an entryway to the otherworld, ready to receive his loosened spirit as he journeys to the witches' sabbat for answers.

~ 👈 ~

Natural bodies of water are blessed with an inherent otherworldly symbolism. Leland (1891) recounts a folktale related to the theme of witches sailing over the sea in eggshells, which may be interpreted as a spirit flight charm of an old variety:

> There was once a gypsy girl who was very clever, and whenever she heard people talk about witches she remembered it well. One day she took an egg-shell and made a small round hole in it very neatly, and

---

[*] Here, the witch consecrates the vessel of water as a "speculum" or magical tool for seeing by calling to the spirits of the Old Ones. Lengthy, Latinate charms using phrases like this one are frequent in the grimoire traditions, including the *Grimorium Verum, Ars Goetia,* and *Greater Key of Solomon.*

ate the yolk and the white, but the shell she put on a heap of white sand by a stream, where it was very likely to be seen. Then she hid herself behind a bush. By and by, when it was night, there came a witch, who, seeing the shell, pronounced a word over it, when it changed to a beautiful boat, into which the witch got and sailed on the water, over the sea.

Water as vehicle appears frequently in witch-lore, and it is echoed by the abundance of folkloric spirit entities said to inhabit the watery depths. These spirits, who are the remnants of prehistoric ancestral worship lying still at the core of modern folk witchcraft, are not all safe or friendly. They are, according to the lore, easily offended, and their subsequent wrath terrible. Some may even be associated with rites of sacrifice practiced by pagan ancestors in their regions:

> In Germany, when a person is drowned, people recollect the fancies of childhood, and exclaim, "The River Spirit claims its yearly sacrifice." Even the hard-reasoning Scotch, years ago, clung to the same superstitious fancy which oftentimes prevented some of the most selfish of their race from saving their drowning fellows. "He will do you an injury if you save him from the water" was one of their fears. In England, too, the north-country people speak of the River Sprite as Jenny Greenteeth, and children dread the green, slimy-covered rocks on the stream's bank or on the brink of a black pool. "Jenny Greenteeth will have thee if thee goest on't river banks" is the warning of a Lancashire mother to her child.

> The Irish fisherman's belief in the Souls'
> Cages and the Merrow, or Man of the Sea, was once
> held in general esteem by the men who earned a
> livelihood on the shores of the Atlantic. This
> Merrow, or Spirit of the Waters, sometimes took
> upon himself a half-human form, and many a sailor
> on the rocky coast of Western Ireland has told the
> tale of how he saw the Merrow basking in the sun,
> watching a storm-driven ship. His form is described
> as half man, half fish, a thing with green hair, long
> green teeth, legs with scales on them, short arms like
> fins, a fish's tail, and a huge red nose. (Green, 1899)

The strong relationship between spirits of witch-kin and bodies of water may be related to the ancient pagan use of bogs as a place of sacrifice and veneration of the dead. Mikanowski (2016) describes one preserved body (the Lindow Man) found in a bog outside Chesire, England, which would have belonged to a man around the year 60 B.C.E. According to experts, he would have been led to the location naked, accompanied by at least two others, then killed in a seated position by a swift blow to the head and simultaneous strangulation and throat laceration, which would have caused "a geyser of blood to erupt from the wound." Scholars are beginning now to view these bodies as the remains of spiritual sacrifice, which links the bog as a body of water to its role as a gate to the otherworld. For the modern folk witch, the spirits of water should be approached with the same care and respect as spirits of the dead.

One of the horned deities sometimes operative within certain branches of folk craft is the Puca (also spelled Bucca or Pookah, depending on the region, most likely derived from the same linguistic root as the former Scottish and Irish spelling). This spirit appears in the lore as a shapeshifting entity frequently taking the form of a black goat or black horse. In Cornish lore, he has two faces: the Bucca Widn (White Bucca) or Bucca Dhu (Black Bucca), associated with benevolence or malevolence, respectively. The Cornish Bucca's relationship with bodies of water is attested by Evans-Wentz' (1911) classic *The Fairy-Faith in Celtic Countries:*

> In this region there are two kinds of pixies, one purely a land-dwelling pixy and the other a pixy which dwells on the sea-strand between high and low water mark. The land-dwelling pixy was usually thought to be full of mischievous fun, but it did no harm. There was a prevalent belief, when I was a boy, that this sea-strand pixy, called Bucca, had to be propitiated by a cast of fish, to ensure the fishermen having a good shot of fish.

The Bucca or Puca, as one of the aspects of the Devil of our craft, appears elsewhere in land-based form, but witches interested in forming relationships with the spirits of water, particularly those operating within Cornish currents, may be well-advised to seek out this Old One.

In the narrated ritual opening this chapter, the witch makes use of the black pot of water as a form of speculum or magical mirror in order to affect a gateway between worlds. This connection between water and mirror is well-attested in our lore and is perhaps one of the oldest connections of bodies of water to our craft. Who among us has not been mesmerized by the reflective properties of a still lake or pond? What witch has never felt the pull of the otherworld near the water's edge, wondering at the mysterious deep beneath its currents? Even Frazier (1922) identifies this connection in his discussion of the lake of Nemi:

> Who does not know Turner's picture of the golden bough? The scene, suffused with the golden glow of imagination in which the divine mind of Turner steeped and transfigured the fairest natural landscape, is a dream-like vision of the little woodland lake of Nemi—"Diana's Mirror," as it was called by the ancients. No one who has seen that calm water, lapped in a green hollow of the Alban hills, can ever forget it...Diana herself might still linger by this lonely shore, still haunt these woodlands wild...For she, too, loved the solitude of the woods and the lonely hills, and sailing overhead on clear nights in the likeness of the silver moon looked down with pleasure on her own fair image reflected on the calm, the burnished surface of the lake, Diana's Mirror.

The speculum itself, most frequently the magical mirror or magician's shew-stone of lore, is described in a variety of grimoiric workings from the early modern and medieval periods in rituals of spirit evocation, serving as a gate between worlds. But what is good for the goose is good for the gander, and a door can open two ways. For the modern folk-witch, the simplicity of the vessel of water consecrated as speculum is rich, and its functionality proven by witches who have experimented with this charm.

In calling to the otherworld upon the surface of the water, we modern witches witness the reflection of our own ancient being, dwelling part in this world and part in the other. Our call upon the water's edge is a small light cast upon the dark and unknown depths of that lake's bottom, and the spirits that answer, those of our ancestry and kin, will aid us in exploring those mysteries.

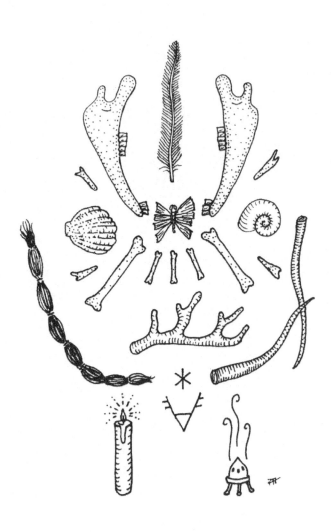

Via Bestium

The May morning is cool around the witch as she sips her honey-sweetened tea. Standing on the old porch, she can smell the sun warming the wet ground, reaching slowly across areas of shadow and condensation as it offers its heat to the night-chilled grass. It smells rich and dark. The little flowers of springtime fields are awake again, and honeybees careen across the land in search of pollen.

The witch has her own work ahead: a task necessary to her learning and growth, to her relationship with the land on which she lives. The powers of witchcraft demand practice, she knows, muscles that must be trained and engaged, and the creatures of the land around her yield their secret mysteries only to those who prove deserving.

Finishing her tea, she steps inside the house to gather items from the cabinet: a bit of antler, dried chamomile flowers, candles, and a palm-sized piece of cleaned, dried honeycomb from the nearby hives last season. She sets the candles, antler, and flowers upon the table in a manner pleasing to her soul, calling to the Old Ones of her craft:

I am of thee, I am of thee—
Come, come, my heart for thee.
I have nothing that is not yours.
Now do I knock upon the door.

She lights the candles and the incense, feeling the presence of those Kings and Queens of old beside her as she sets to her task. The witch holds a bit of honeycomb in her hand, lifting it up to the candlelight for close inspection. It is golden yellow, illuminated from behind, fragile as paper. She closes her eyes to gently feel her way across its ridged, hexagonal patterns. With her witch-sight, she perceives the lingering currents of life there: she sees the colony that built its walls and cells with tiny mouths, piece by delicate piece. This was once a part of their queendom. She hears their hum, charged and incessant, a bright droning that shakes the air around her. The vibration builds and fills her bones like a wild music. She begins to tilt her head and move her arms, subtly at first, like an antenna shifting to attune to some hidden signal.

Into the shape of a bee I go
with blackest shout and blackest throw,
and I shall go in Our Lady's name
until I come home again. *

---

* The charm here is adapted from Scottish witch Isobel Gowdie in 1662, who provides it in its original form as a transmutation formula for becoming a hare.

The witch inhales deeply and slowly, concentrating on her powers of perception, feeling deeply into the currents of the hive that built the comb. The honey in her tea still courses through her, its sharp, stinging sweetness still on her tongue. She speaks the words again, this time more slowly, with authority, feeling each syllable bend around her tongue:

Into the shape of a bee I go…

Finally, she feels her fetch—her otherworldly shadow-double—respond modestly, with a single twitch. It is the shadow of a segmented leg. She wills it further, producing from her own shadow more legs, followed by wings, fur, a segmented abdomen, and those complex eyes like stained glass that are a hallmark of the insect world.

And I shall go in Our Lady's name…

The witch is only vaguely aware that she has lifted her arms by her sides, moving them slowly, as if in dance, twisting her wrist to mimic the movements of the spirit form she seeks.

At last, she feels it is ready: her fetch-form is fully shaped by the charm. As she opens her mouth to exhale, she feels her consciousness pulled into a smaller spirit-form that rests on her tongue. Her body feels its small legs walking across her tongue's surface, and with her witch senses, she can also feel the wetness of the tongue against her many legs. With one more step, she will be ready to depart. Exhaling long and slow, she moves her spirit out of her own mouth and over her teeth, experiencing the room through the form of her fetch, hovering around her body still posturing before the working space and the lit candles, diving towards the window, and flying onward, to the mysteries that await. What she learns on this journey will be brought back to improve her craft, to shape many workings to come. Her physical body waits there, guarded by her familiars and the Old Ones, for her safe and careful return.

~ 🖎 ~

Transmogrification—the art of shifting one's spirit into that of an animal form—is a hallmark of oldest craft that is well-attested in lore and history. Like flight as a whole, however, practitioners of modern witchcraft understand that these charms affect consciousness and spirit form, enabling us to experience worlds and understandings accessible only to the creatures of our lands.

Thompson (1929) describes the various attempts of officials to curtail the remnants of pagan shapeshifting practices in the early years of the church:

> In the fifth century, St. Maximus of Turin exclaims: 'What is it but frantic folly when men, created by God and in the image of God, transform themselves to herd animals or to wild beasts or to some

monstrous shape?' St. Peter Chrysologus enjoins that Christians should strive to convert 'all who have masqueraded in the likeness of animals, who have metamorphosed themselves as draught cattle, who have assumed the shape of herd animals, who have turned themselves into devils.' In the sixth century, St. Caesarius of Arles is as emphatic: 'Is there any sensible man, who could ever believe that there are actually rational individuals willing to put on the appearance of a stag and transform themselves into wild beasts? Some dress themselves in the skins of herd animals; others put on the heads of horned beasts; swelling and wildly exulting if only they can so completely metamorphose themselves into the animal kind that seem to have entirely abandoned the human shape.'

The pointed loathing of church officials towards the transmogrification rituals here reveals something else in its wording; that these rites were viewed as being connected intimately with the Devil, that figure being himself a connecting thread between the human sorcerer and the beast of the hunt.

The infamous Scottish witch Isobel Gowdie described charms of transformation most famously into the forms of hare and cat (Wilby, 2010). Her own charms have been adapted and utilized by folk and traditional witches with much success, the original version for shapeshifting into a hare being as follows:

I shall go into a hare,

> *With sorrow and sych and meickle care;*
> *And I shall go in the Devil's name,*
> *Ay while I come home again.*

"Sych" has been interpreted as "sigh" or "sighing," while "meickle" here should be read as something similar to "much." When she determined that it was time to assume her human form, she would use the following charm:

> *Hare, hare, God send thee care.*
> *I am in a hare's likeness now,*
> *But I shall be in a woman's likeness even*
> *now.*

While spoken charms are part of a living, flexible discipline of our art, the choice of words in Gowdie's version here does matter. Gowdie's choice of a hare is echoed many times over in the witch-lore of Western Europe, perhaps owing in no small part to the hare's ties to the cycles of the seasons and its ability to pass into tunnels beneath the surface of the earth. In assuming the form of the animal, she calls on the Devil; in assuming human form, she calls on God. This ability to call on both God and the Devil in oscillation is a hallmark of old folk craft and a testament to folk witchcraft as a flexible spiritual tradition that mingles easily with elements of dominant religion. Most interesting, perhaps, is that Gowdie's returning charm does not imply a return to a "true form," but intentionally conjures the "likeness" of a woman, a recognition of the witch's soul as something other than human or hare, but beyond both, wearing each as a kind of convenient disguise when required. The wisdom in Gowdie's wording here emphasizes the witch's otherworldly nature. *All spirit forms—which is to say ways of perceiving the self—are, in fact, illusions* when we understand the broader implications of consciousness as a malleable tool in our craft.

In addition to the hare form utilized by Gowdie, the toad has a long traditional association with witchcraft and shapeshifting. Leland (1891) observes that the toad "plays a prominent part in gypsy (as in other) witchcraft, which it may well do, since in most Romany dialects there is the same word for *toad* or *frog*, and the *devil*." He goes on to provide an example of such toad-shifting in witch-lore in the form of a recorded tale:

> You know, sir, that people who live out of doors all the time, as we do, see and know a great deal about such creatures. One day we went to a farmhouse, and found the wife almost dying because she thought she was bewitched by a woman who came every day in the form of a great toad to her door and looked in. And, sure enough, while she was talking the toad came, and the woman was taken in such a way with fright that I thought she'd have died...Then we caught the toad, and tied the shears so as to make a cross—you see!—and with it threw the toad into the

fire, and poured the salt on it. So the witchcraft was
ended, and the lady gave us a good meal and ten
shillings.

The common toad's association with witches,
which has its roots in the toad's symbolic ties to
natural cycles, poisoning, and the ability to move
"between worlds" via land or water, has
unfortunately ended in many an innocent
creature's gruesome end. I will not here recount
the multitude of charms related to killing toads in
cruel, excruciating ways and collecting various
bones and organs from them for magical use.
Witches today should know better.

Charms of transmogrification can, like
many other gates of spirit flight, be combined with
the use of salves and ointments. Apuleius' classic
text *The Golden Ass*, written sometime in the 2nd
century, describes the transformation of the witch
Pamphile using an ointment:

> ...about the first watch of the night she led me,
> walking a-tiptoe and very softly, into that high
> chamber, and bade me look through the chink of a
> door. Where first I saw how Pamphile put off all her
> garments, and took out of a certain coffer sundry
> kind of boxes, of which she opened one and
> tempered the ointment therein with her fingers, and
> then rubbed her body therewith from the sole of the
> foot to the crown of the head: and when she had
> spoken much privily with the lamp, she shaked all
> the parts of her body, and as they gently moved

behold I perceived a plume of feathers did burgeon
out upon them, strong winds did grow, her nose was
more crooked and hard, her nails turned into claws,
and so Pamphile became an owl: then she cried and
screeched like a bird of that kind, and willing to
prove her force, moved herself from the ground by
little and little, till at last she leaped up and flew
quite away. (Gaselee & Adlington, 1915)

What words the witch whispers to her lamp (or
candle) in this description is perhaps best answered
by the living body of witches practicing today.
There is, of course, more than one answer. As a
mythic tale, *The Golden Ass* draws on folklore and
poetic license, but we must understand as modern
witches that here, Apuleius is recounting a
common motif of witch-lore. Nor should the
perceptions of onlookers be discredited
necessarily, since the perception of forms can be
affected by both fumes given off of certain plants
and the consciousness-bending properties of
rituals themselves in the right context.

The modern lore of the werewolf,
considered in the popular imagination to be a
separate canon altogether from witchcraft,
actually has its roots in the shapeshifting traditions
of our art. In the medieval period, hunts for
werewolves took on the same mass hysteria as the
witch-hunts, and those convicted were often
believed to have possessed talismans or knowledge
of charms for transforming into the wolf form.

Scot (1584) recounts the common belief that witches "speciallie transubstantiate themselves into wolves" in order to devour innocent Christians.

In Celtic lore, we see in the Welsh manuscript of the *Hanes Taliesin* (mid-16th century) the significance of transmogrification in this myth tradition. Gwion, after accidentally tasting three drops of magical liquid from the cauldron of Ceridwen, fled from her in various animal forms:

> I fled with vigour, I fled as a frog;
> I fled in the semblance of a raven, scarcely finding rest;
> I fled vehemently, I fled as a chain;
> I fled as a roe in an entangled thicket;
> I fled as a wolf cub, I fled as a wolf in a wilderness;
> I fled as a thrush, the interpreter of omens;
> I fled as a fox, leaping and turning;
> I fled as a marten, which did not avail;
> I fled as a squirrel, that vainly hides;
> I fled as an antlered stag of free course;
> I fled as iron in a glowing fire;
> I fled as a spear-head, woe to him who desires it;
> I fled as a bull fierce in fighting;
> I fled as a bristly boar seen in a ravine... (Nash, 1858)

When at last he becomes a grain of corn, she becomes a black hen and swallows him, thus becoming pregnant with him as her child, and eventually giving birth to him. The pagan symbolism preserved here is difficult to understand in a modern context, but Ceridwen's chase illustrates the interdependence inherent in the web of life. It is Gwion's newfound understanding of the art of magic that allows him to step outside his body, to experience existence in an interconnected web of life. Their chase mimics the predator-prey cycles of complex ecosystems, the ways creatures of the land and sea and sky are dependent on one another to exist, and in many ways, *only* exist in connection with one another. Ceridwen, of course, in addition to being a Celtic goddess associated with transformation and rebirth, is one of the oldest mythic sorceresses in our lore. Her name, etymologically, renders "crooked woman" or "bent woman," an ancient prototype of the very image of the wise and powerful witch tending her cauldron.

The language rendered here to narrate the transformative journey of Taliesin is echoed in folk-magical charms such as the Scottish "fath fith," which is, depending on the intention and the charmer, useful for concealment or transmogrification into animal forms. Carmichael (1900) provides a version of this charm:

Fath-fith
Will I make on thee,
By Mary of the augury,
By Bride of the corslet,
From sheep, from ram,
From goat, from buck,
From fox, from wolf,

From sow, from boar,
From dog, from cat,
From hipped-bear,
From wilderness-dog,
From watchful scan,
From cow, from horse,
From bull, from heifer,
From daughter, from son,
From the birds of the air,
From the creeping things of the earth,
From the fishes of the sea,
From the imps of the storm.

We see both in the listing feature, which is itself a hypnotic device of this charm, and in the rapid series of animal forms mentioned, how the threads of the old lore and charms arrange and rearrange themselves together. Folk craft's organic flexibility and natural variation allow us to spot the pattern of common elements defining the heart of the charm, the mechanism that captures its potency.

Most important, perhaps, to the witch-lore of shapeshifting arts are the mysteries coalesced and preserved in the image of the Devil himself. In medieval witch-lore, which is inseparable from folk-religious influence, the Devil can be understood as the first shape-shifter in the world due to his transformation into a serpent in Genesis. Although the text does not actually name the serpent as Satan or Samael, it is a folkloric belief that the Devil took on the likeness of a serpent in order to tempt Eve with forbidden knowledge. As a catalyst figure, the Devil, in this story, is actually responsible for the maturation of the first humans and the eventual development of human intellect and all of civilization itself.

Approached historically, we can understand the symbolism of the Devil (as a half-human, half-quadruped figure) as a union of the human and animal worlds. This communion of two worlds of being is central to animistic spiritual practices around the world, which is perhaps why some of the oldest images of what we now call the Devil are also identified by archaeologists as depictions of shamans wearing animal skins and headdresses in order to take on the powers and vibrancy of the animal world. The most famous of these images is undoubtedly the cave painting known as "The Sorcerer," which was painted and chiseled into rock around 13,000 B.C.E. in a cave in France. Thompson's (1929) *The History of the Devil, or, The Horned God of the West*, asserts the fundamental connection between our modern image of the Devil and these ancient images of what are truly the first sorcerers of Western Europe, the first masters of our art, and those from whom all of today's witches are in some way descended. In mastering the shapeshifting arts, witches walk in these footsteps, learning perhaps only a fraction of the Devil's (i.e., the first sorcerer's) hidden craft.

In beginning transmogrification work, it will serve the witch well to look inwardly at her own nature when deciding which creatures to work with. Not all personalities are compatible with all creatures. For example, some witches (myself included) connect more easily with creatures that hunt than with creatures that scavenge and gather. I have always loved cats for their independence, their keen senses, and their intelligence. The behavior of the creature you seek first should speak to you on a personal level. While there is much to be learned from shapeshifting work with creatures that we fear, those barriers are more difficult to cross and are probably best suited to advanced practitioners who make transmogrification a regular part of their personal practice. Much like the witch in the charm narrative at the beginning of this chapter, it is helpful and recommended to procure (always by ethical means) a bit of the animal itself: either its shell, bone, hair, tooth, or a bit of its nest or dwelling. This aids the witch in connecting with the creature's unique imprint and nature.

Via Imaginibus

In the hall, the grandfather clock strikes midnight, and so the witch fetches the necessary tools to achieve the sabbatic ekstasis required for the work this night: an old cigar box—the "skilly box" of old cunning craft—containing herbs for fumigation, a plain candle, dried moss, the neatly folded skin of a serpent, and the cards of art. These cards are not the gaudy, iridescent tarots of today, but a faithful rendition of the 1804 Tarocco di Marsiglia, complete with its softly gazing moon and beastly, wonderfully colorful Devil. The witch knows that the type of card matters to the charm this night.

Sitting at the dining room table, the witch arranges the altar of plant and animal matter, laying the skin between the bits of dried moss, and lighting the candle that will represent the light of between the Devil's horns. They produce several cards from the deck, setting them before the arrangement on the table in a neat little pile. It is time.

First, the witch sets the Devil, calling softly, as if whispering a song to the candle's flame:

> As the witches of old did call you,
> so, too, do I call you, Devil of Art.
> I offer you this candle and this incense.[*]

Next, the witch sets The Moon, overlapping slightly with the first card:

> And thou, bright Moon,
> first mother of our craft,
> come to light the path.

The third card set against the first two is The Fool:

> Wandering wild one, child of Cain, come.

The final card is now set so that the bottom edge of the four cards form a wheel, a rotation, with a diamond-shaped gap in the center:

> And thou, Fortuna, who moves The World
> as a wandering globe beneath your feet,
> come, come, come.

> I conjure not four cards[†], but four keepers,

---

[*] Isabela Bellochio, in 1589, described lighting a candle to the Devil's image in the trump card of the tarot.

[†] The phrasing here is adapted from a charm to conjure Laverna via a cartomantic operation recorded in Leland's (1899) *Aradia*. In charms like this one, the cards must be named as their referents verbally to emphasize their role as simulacrum.

four locksmiths, four stewards, four powers
to open the gate between the worlds.

Placing hands upon either side of the arrangement, the witch gazes into the space between the cards, breathing deeply, readying for the essay. They feel their spirit loosen by the combination of candlelight, fumigation, and words of craft. The Old Ones are pulling the witch to them again, to attend their revels in the otherworld, to partake of their wisdom and nourishment, to learn and to grow in mastery. Slowly, the witch begins the age-old chant of transvection to depart through the gate between the cards:

Thout a tout tout,
throughout and about—[*]

They begin chanting faster and faster in a hushed breath, careful to annunciate each syllable. The repetition of the *T* consonant, at an exaggerated speed, forms a kind of percussion, a cacophony like the echo of footsteps in another room. The witch feels the ecstasy of their loosening spirit, and at the moment of crescendo, exhales long and fully, stretching their mouth open to release their spirit through the gate between the worlds, to attend the old teachers, to attend the old feast, the invisible rite as ancient as the first sorcerers who dared to reach into forbidden realms.

---

[*] This incantatory formula is provided in Joseph Glanvill's 1681 *Saducismus Triumphatus*, in which he records the charms and lore of witches in various traditions across Europe.

~ 🖎 ~

Despite the attempts of fanatical religious movements throughout the history of Western Christianity, images—whether as paintings, illustrations in books, cards, sculptures, or stained glass—were as evocative to our ancestors as they are to witches today. While the written word in published books can be constrained by puritanical laws, the image is more difficult to hinder. Some of our oldest understandings of the concepts of our pagan ancestors come through images, whether as cave paintings, the illustrations in banned magical books, or the fragments of art left among the ruins of our ancestors. The image allows us to see, even for a moment, what another mind sees.

Perhaps this is part of why religious authorities were so resistant to the spreading popularity of tarot and other forms of playing cards in the early modern period. We know that in 1589, Isabela Bellochio was accused of witchcraft in the form of lighting a candle before the "devil and the tarots" (Martin, 1989). Leland's (1899) *Aradia or the Gospel of the Witches* describes cartomancy specifically as a gift given to those who follow the path of witchcraft. We also know that John Northbrooke, in 1519, described playing cards as "an invention of the Devil" (Jackson, 2016). It was, of course, not long before the famous term "the devil's picturebook" rose to popularity as a way to describe the contents of both playing and tarot cards (for tarot cards were, from the beginning, designed to be played in games). Jones (1584) recounts a dicer's description of the making of cards:

> Insomuch on a time I heard a distemperate dicer solemnly sweare, yet he faithfully believed, the dice were first made of the bones of a witch, cards of her skin, in which there hath ever since remained an enchantment, ye whosoever once taketh delight in either, he shall never have power utterly to leave them...

Clearly, the association of witches and the Devil with card games has left a lasting impression, yielding a wealth of folklore and superstition for the shrewd witch to utilize in charm work. My previous work, *Cartomancy in Folk Witchcraft*, explores these arts in greater detail.

Huson (1971) offers an insightful explanation here of why the images in tarot cards can be understood as a key to transvection work in the cartomantic arts:

> ...the entire mystery cycle of the pagan initiate's triumphs came to be paralleled in the Christian myth...a fusion of these cults typical of syncretist thinking...Originally these initiations may have been purely mundane, such as the experience of love. But centuries added to the mystery. To the

medieval occultist, the trumps undoubtedly
contained all sorts of occult powers, for by their
mythological associations many of them shared
common symbols with magical notae, which, as we
have seen, were talismans in their own right.

Much like folk witchcraft incorporated elements
of Catholicism into its magical charms and
operations, the tarot, though originally devised as
a simple game, seems to have preserved a
syncretism between pagan mythical figures and the
cosmology of Christianity. Its images offer
witches past and present a thread connecting us to
our pagan roots. Its objectification of powerful
elements like Death and The World, which can be
held in the witch's hand, dealt on the table, hidden,
or cast aside, suggest a play at performing the role
of deity in the context of a mere game, the
deification of the player herself.

Similar to the images preserved in cards,
the simple labyrinth has enjoyed a long history and
a resurgence of modern usage among traditional
witches. The Rock Valley Labyrinth carvings in
Cornwall have been dated as old as 4,000 B.C.E.,
and the cross-style labyrinth formation they
feature is echoed across Celtic countries. The
Christian tradition of walking along labyrinths in
prayer and religious meditation no doubt evolved
from the practices of pagan ancestors for whom
the following of the labyrinth's path would have
represented a kind of spiritual journey.

Practitioners of folk craft today enjoy using small, hand-held labyrinth carvings, sometimes called "labyrinth stones" or "finger labyrinths," which can be traced with the finger to assist the practitioner in achieving a trance-like state conducive to meditation or ekstasis.

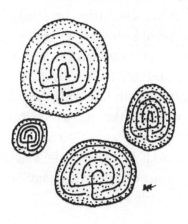

Images potent for spirit flight are invariably those tied to ancestral or personal memory, connecting this art to practices of renaissance occultists such as Giordano Bruno, author of the 1582 *Ars Memoriae (The Art of Memory)* and the 1591 *De Imaginum, Signorum et Idearum Compositione (On the Composition of Images, Signs, and Ideas)*. Bruno devised intricate sigils designed to capture disciplinary memory and intricate geocentric models illustrating the layout of the universe itself. The concept of ars memoria itself is older than Bruno, however, finding its root in ancient philosophy and the engaging of senses through visualized locations that the practitioner has experienced before.

For folk and traditional witches, the complexity of Bruno's formulae are impressive and informative, but unnecessary in practical application. Our ancestors practicing animistic spirit work would not have used such ornate concepts to explain their work, and neither need we. A simple and reliable formula for spirit flight via imaginibus, one in line with the folk practices of witches of old, makes use of a natural location in the practitioner's own region. This is in line with 17th century witch Isobel Gowdie's description of her spiritual journey under the familiar landscape of the Dounie Hills:

> Yet she had been, she said, in the Dounie Hills, and got meat there from the Queen of Fairies more than she could eat. She added, that the queen is bravely clothed in white linen and in white and brown cloth, that the King of Fairy is a brave man; and there were elf-bulls roaring and skoilling at the entrance of their palace, which frightened her much.

The ancient location described here is known today as Dounie Hill Fort, being constructed over 2,000 years ago.

While ancient burial sites and settlements can be ideal for modern witches to practice spirit flight via imaginibus, places with natural passageways are fertile as well. The location can feature an old tree with a gaping hole in its trunk, an entrance to a cave, an old stone well, a sinkhole, or even a body of water. When visiting the location, the witch should commit as many details to memory as possible, engaging all senses. What does the air smell like? How does the grass feel? What noises can be heard in the distance? Later, in a ritual setting, the witch can conjure the image of the place, and proceed to move his spirit through the passageway as a point of entry to the otherworld.

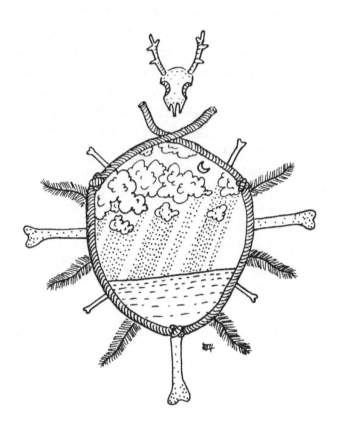

Via Tempestatis

Thunder shakes the air outside the witch's home. She feels the vibrations of the storm in the floorboards of the house, rippling up from the earth beneath like drums. A cacophony of wind and rain batters the windows. Yet the witch knows that behind this frightening display of power is an opportunity for craft.

Stepping outside of her door, the witch breathes deeply the familiar scent of petrichor—that chemical released by rainwater hitting the soil for miles around. She gazes across the horizon, committing the scene to memory: sheets of rain blur the line of trees while blue-gray undulations of cloud roll across the sky, coiling as they go.

Feeling the cool wet under her feet, the witch focuses on her body, allowing the rain to pelt her skin, becoming one with the storm, allowing it to wash over her, permitting herself to feel its force completely. The power of the tempest is a living thing, she knows, and one that must be savored when the opportunity presents itself.

Later, this potent force will be put to use in her art. The power of the storm, passed through her body, will be focused and bound into a string of knots, an age-old method for storing the force of wind for magical use. To do this, the feeling of a living storm, the immediate sensation of it, must first be captured, then focused through the witch's hands in the ritualistic act of knotting. The power stored now will be bound up later in the charm—one to be used to ride the gale to the hidden feast, to participate in that loving and dread company at the sabbat.

Upon the night of her flight to come, the witch will walk to her place of power, her collection of bones and spirit vessels upon her altar. She will light the candle of those old spirits and call them to her—

> Eko, Eko, Azarak—
> Eko, Eko, Zomelak—
> Zod Ru Koz e, Zod Ru Koo—
> Zod Ru Goz e, Goo Ru Moo—
> Eko, Eko, Hiu, Hiu, Hiu...[*]

Dragging her forked staff in a circle about herself, she will bless the space about her as a waypoint between the worlds—

> Here do I set the ring about,
> Thout a Thout and Tout a Tout.

---

[*] This conjuration, popularized by Doreen Valiente and Gerald Gardner, actually finds its published source in a J. F. C. Fuller article printed in 1921 in the *Form* journal, which was edited by the infamous sorcerer Austin Osman Spare. The author offers no original source, unfortunately. Posch (2016) offers a possible source for this chant in archaic Arabic. "Al-Zaraq" renders "the blue one," while "zhamal-uka" could mean "your beauty." This linguistic analysis suggests a connection to Mal'ak Tawus, the Peacock Angel, who has a strong folkloric connection to Lucifer.

Reaching across the abyss between this world and the next, she will call the four winds to aid her, just as the witches of the old lore called to the them—

> *Boreas, where art thou? Come.*
> *Eurus, where art thou? Come.*
> *Notus, where art thou? Come.*
> *Zephyrus, where art thou? Come.* [*]
> *Bind these winds into such knots of art*
> *that I might use in my craft.*

With her witch-sight, she will perceive the power of the storm stored in her very body, hovering around her skin. She will pull it gently so as not to lose the thread, guiding it into her hand to set into the knotted cord, one knot at a time, each charged to hold the potency until the hour of need.

One day, perhaps soon, perhaps months from now, the sabbat will beckon. The witch will feel that familiar pull to attend the hidden rites of the otherworld. On that night, she will fetch her witch-knots, artfully made, and unlock one or more—depending on the need—to conjure the spiritual power of the gale to carry her. She will feel that same thunder crackle around her, that same pelt of rain against her face. She will allow the current of the storm's

---

[*] These are the old names of the four winds to the classical sorcerers of ancient Greece. The questioning of the spirit with "Where art thou?" is an incantatory theme of renaissance grimoires along with the garbled Latin "Quod tardis?" (Why do you delay?).

magic to envelop her body, lifting her spirit from her physical form, riding the tempest to the hallowed otherworldly rites, to return again to her body and dwelling with wisdom and with power.

~ 🖎 ~

The image of the witch riding the storm conjures folkloric descriptions of Nicneven, Scottish witch-queen and goddess of craft, as described in Walter Scott's (1830) *Letters on Demonology and Witchcraft—*

> It was from the same source [referring to Celtic and Northern pagan lore] also, in all probability, that additional legends were obtained, of a gigantic and malignant female, the Hecate of this mythology, who rode on the storm, and marshalled the rambling host of wanderers under her grim banner. This hag...was called Nicneven in that later system which blended the faith of the Celts and of the Goths on this subject. The great Scottish poet Dunbar has made a spirited description of this Hecate riding at the head of witches and good neighbors (fairies, namely), sorceresses and elves, indifferently, upon the ghostly eve of All-Hallow Mass.

The name *Nicneven* comes from the Scottish Gaelic *Neachneohain*, which is usually translated as "daughter of power" or "daughter of divinity." Syncretists would accept this connection between her and Hecate, while reconstructionists would prefer to keep them separate. In any case, we can recognize certain similarities between the two, and it is perfectly legitimate to approach Nicneven as a deific witch-queen who at least occupies the same cosmological category as the triform goddess. Confusingly for those outside of folk craft, the name Nicneven is also given to an accused witch in Scottish history. This connection is best understood as a testament to the living animism that is an inextricable part of folk craft; our Old Ones were once masters of craft themselves, risen to greatness in death, and over many lifetimes, their names and images became themselves deific. Their names are the names of deities, the names of the dead, and the names of ancestors all in one.

It should come as no surprise that the figure of Nicneven is associated with storm-riding; throughout history, witch-lore has referred to the abilities of our people to use wind and storm in craft. Famously, the witches of North Berwick rallied to conjure a tempest that would overwhelm the royal ships of King James and prevent his journey to Scotland (Stuart, 1597). Though James did land in Scotland, the storm terrified the company and crew and caused many onboard to fear for their lives.

Any lore-based discussion of weather magic in Western Europe would be remiss if it did not include the tempestarii, sorcerers fabled to "raise the storm" by magical means. This group of practitioners was denounced by Charlemagne's laws in the same breath as witches:

> No doubts were entertained of it in Europe. Agobardus, bishop of Leyden, says of his neighborhood, 'Almost every one in these districts, high and low, citizens, peasants, old and young, credit that hail and thunder are produced through the means of mankind. For, immediately hearing the thunder, or beholding the lightning, they say, 'the storm is raised'; but when interrogated what they mean by 'the storm being raised,' some with little hesitation, as usual with the ignorant, declare, that it is from the incantations of those persons called *tempestarii*, and utter execrations against them. (Dalyell, 1834)

We can view this folkloric thread connecting weather-lore in Western Europe to the role of witches in aiding or preventing the growth of crops, the success of individual farms, and the overall thriving or failing of local economies that would have relied on ship traffic. The elements of nature that are outside the powers of society have, since time immemorial, been ascribed to those powers of the "other," be they named *sorcerer, enchantress, fae,* or *witch.*

Moreover, the lore of weather-witching is catalogued in a variety of early modern texts, including Guazzo's (1608) *Compendium Maleficarum*:

> It is most clearly proved by experience that witches

can control not only the rain and the hail and the wind, but even the lightning when God permits. Therefore Andrea Cesalpino, in his *Daemonum investigation peripatetica*, says that men have been known who could raise, not only hail storms, but lightning also...They can also evoke darkness; wherefore we read in Marco Polo that the Tartars are so potent in devilish illusions that they can cause darkness when and where they will, and that he once narrowly escaped the robbers through the projection of this art.

Even Leland's (1899) folkloric collection *Aradia, or, Gospel of the Witches* includes an interesting tale of a follower of Diana who manipulates the wind to overthrow her oppressors. In the tale, a young woman is fated by her parents to join a nunnery, but desires the love of a husband and a family instead. By praying to Diana, she is able to secure a handsome young suitor, but her mother delivers her to the church authorities to be locked in a tower for her crimes of witchcraft. In a dramatic scene, a storm overwhelms the structure, freeing her and tearing the building to the ground:

> ...and standing by the door of the house, which is still there, [she] prayed in the light of the full moon to Diana, that she might be delivered from the dire persecution to which she had been subjected, since even her own parents had willingly given her over to an awful death.
>
> Now her parents and the priests, and all who sought

her death, were in the palace watching lest she escape.

When lo! in answer to her prayer there came a terrible tempest and overwhelming wind, a storm such as man had never seen before, which overthrew and swept away the palace with all who were in it; there was not one stone left upon another, nor one soul alive of all who were there. The gods had replied to the prayer.

Much like the use of poisonous unguents or shapeshifting charms, however, the command of storm and wind in the witch's art is somewhat different from its portrayals in folklore and superstition. The lore preserves the spirit of the thing, the seed of truth to be offered to future generations. It does not generally offer concrete methodology. For this, we turn to elements of folk magic, as in the tradition of weather magic by witch's knots:

Higden says of the Isle of Man, 'In that Ilonde is sortilege and witchcrafte vsed: for women there, sell to shipmen, wynde, as it were closed vnder thre knots of threde, so that the more wynde he wold have, the more knots he must vndo'...By the northern nations, the Finns and Laplanders, 'three knots were cast on a leathern thong. Moderate breezes attended the loosening of the one; stronger gales the next, and vehement tempests, even with thunder, in ancient times, followed the loosening of the third.' These knotted thongs were sold to navigators. (Dalyell, 1834)

Although most of us today have no need of raising wind in a ship's sails, the modern folk witch, ever seeking the practical application of elder charms and superstitions in the craft, would do well to note the heart of these knotting charms—that the power of the storm can be by this art caught and stored for future use, so that the witch need not wait for the necessary weather when seeking flight via tempestatis.

The traditions of witch-flight via tempestatis offer us much insight into the inherent power and symbolism of the storm. Just as the clouds and currents of that world careen over our own, so too do the currents of the otherworld pass through and over our mortal world. In seeking the magic of the winds, witches, rather than commanding and subjugating that power, allow ourselves to be swept away in its rapture, growing closer to the otherworldly current that is, at its core, what sets us apart from the world around us.

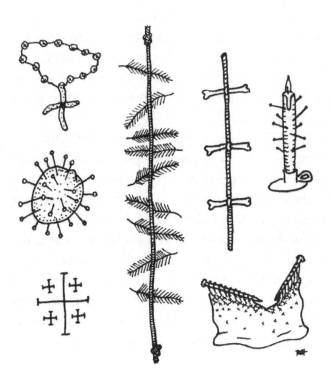

Via Repetitio

It is an age-old charm, one the witch has relied on over years of practice, perfecting over the cumulation of time. Just as his ancestors did. When he performs it, he can feel their presence, their history, the collision of the old pagan magic and the new folk religion, the steeping of those ancient leaves of practice in the new waters of the church. Not the church of today, but the church hundreds of years ago, its Latinate incantations adapted and arranged to suit the magical needs of the common people, its lofty rituals incorporated into the witch's arts in order to tap into the growing reservoir of power behind those acts.

Lighting a single candle in his bedroom, the witch begins the working of the charm:

Io Regina Pigmeorum. Dark Queen.
Io Dominus Umbrarum. Lord of Shadows.
Come to the call. Come to your child.

He sets the fumigation to light—a smudge of blended herbs chosen for their pleasing fragrance—and wafts it over the *candle, its smoke coiling and rising in shifting forms over the soft light.*

> *Open for me the hidden gate,*
> *that I may gain the knowledge I seek this night.*

Now begins the heart of the charm: the repetition of old words until the tongue bends around them, until the senses are arrested, until the rhythms of language become the drum-beat beckoning the spirit into the otherworld. Its formulae are tried and true. The witch begins slowly, with a simple string of beads in hand, a length ending not in a rosary's crucifix, but in a tied knot of black horse hair, representing that dread lord of the sabbat and ancient teacher, the Man in Black, the Devil himself, the first sorcerer and master of the art, the one who can open the gate to that ethereal enclave of hidden craft. Each bead in the length will be pinched between thumb and knuckle of forefinger, each one representing a single repetition of the charm hundreds of years old:

> *I rode a gray horse.*
> *It is called a gray mare.*
> *Gray mane, gray tail,*
> *gray stripe down its back*
> *and not a hair on it*
> *that was not coal-black.* [*]

---

[*] The lines here are adapted from the ballad *Nottamun Town*, an American Appalachian folk song brought over originally by immigrants from the British Isles. The speaker in this song journeys to the otherworld through

The witch knows the secret to the work is focusing the attention on the tip of the tongue and the cadence of the voice, as if speaking to someone directly within the candle's flame. Muttering incantations to oneself is pointless. The crux of the charm is in speaking to and for the hidden power which hears, bending the voice pleasingly to the otherworld, calling to and for those dread powers, the incantatory formulae crashing over the hidden listener like waves.

> *I rode a gray horse...*
> *It is called a gray mare...*

As he repeats the charm, losing count, allowing the beads to become the only real measure of time around him, the witch begins to lose himself in the pattern. His voice feels other to him know, the syllables strange, the words not his own. He becomes both speaker and listener at once, experiencing the flow of the incantation like an onlooker, placed outside himself.

It is in this state of ekstasis that he begins to perceive what he has been waiting for, a blackness that envelops his senses. His eyes closed, he is now able to perceive with his witch-sight a single door standing alone in the darkness, its surface wooden and rough, its latch worn from centuries of use. Behind him, he hears his own voice echoing with the repetition of the charm, its syllables bouncing off of stone walls from some far-away room.

---

the performance of impossible tasks, eventually meeting a procession people who "never were born," being led by a King and Queen.

Slowly, the witch knocks upon the door. He knows that the powers waiting on the other side are neither heavenly nor infernal, neither angels nor demons, but older and wiser than both. They could be cruel or kind as they please, and for this reason, they demand respect. Beneath his mingled fear and excitement, the witch perceives the other and most important feeling: that of love and belonging. This is the gate to the otherworld that is his true and only home, to that hidden assembly that is his true source, his most ancient family, his parents and siblings in the otherworld, gathered together in the ecstatic covine of the true sabbat. The latch slowly turns, and the gap of darkness beyond the door grows. He perceives the faint light of torches and voices in wild revelry. Opening the ancient door, the witch steps inside.

~ 🖘 ~

It is difficult, if not impossible to overstate the role of repetitious or counting charms in folk witchcraft. The meditative properties of repetitive acts and their potent effect on consciousness has been recognized throughout history in our lore, and such charms are among our most prized for their utter practicality and ease of use in achieving ecstatic states necessary to our art. Our ancestors— whether by cunning craft, fairy-doctoring, brujeria, stregheria, or herb-doctoring (or any of the other ancestral branches of our art)—favored counting and repetitious charms for good reason.

Perhaps the most infamous of these is the witch's ladder, which remains a popular charm to this very day. Far from being a paradigm of singular practice, the witch's ladder actually embodies a diverse array of similar charms preserved in folk traditions in different cultures. In 1887, Colles noted the discovery of a witch's ladder in a hidden attic room of a house in Somerset which was inaccessible from the interior of the home. Several brooms were discovered there, as well as a length of braided cord with feathers "woven into it" at regular intervals. His descriptions and illustration were published in *The Folk-Lore Journal.* Though Colles noted the presence of "white witches" operating in the area, he mistakenly identifies these practitioners are separate altogether from what he called "black witchcraft," which he described as a dying art. It is of course obvious to any folk witch today that such distinctions serve only to avoid persecution from locals, and that Colles would most likely have found similar knotted or braided charms in the homes of any of his supposed "white witches" as well.

Braided and knotted charms are present in folk magic and lore of other countries as well. Leland (1892) documented the role of the witch's ladder in Italy, and even provides a transcribed discussion with a local of the time:

> ...There was in Florence four years ago a child which was bewitched. It pined away. The parents took it to all the shrines in vain, and it died.
>
> Some time after something hard was felt in the bed on which the child had slept. They opened the bed and found what is called a *guirlanda della strege*, or witches' garland. It is made by taking the cord and tying knots in it. While doing this pluck feathers one by one from a living hen, and stick them into the knots, uttering a malediction with every one...

Leland connects this charm to similar braiding charms involving black or colored threads, which are also described as useful in malediction:

> Take the hairs of the person, or else the stockings, and those not clean, for there must be in them his or her perspiration. Then with black and red thread sew the stockings one across the other. And if you have the hairs of the person, make them a *guirlands unita con stoppa*—a cord spun with flax or hemp—then take the feathers and *si cuopre questa robba*—you cover (or work up) this thing in the form of a hen, and, taking the feathers, work or weave them with black and red thread...

Though the more malicious repetitious charms of knotting and braiding (maleficium) have gathered more attention in the public eye over the years, there is nothing essential to the symbolic act of knotting or braiding that ties malevolence to this manner of charm. Indeed, repetitious corded charms, much like the poppet or human simulacrum, have been and still today are used to effect benevolent aid and all manner of workings, including the achievement transcendent states of consciousness.

It is important to understand this tradition in both English and Scottish cunning craft currents as tied to the unseated legacy of Catholicism in the British Isles. The use of rosaries, which were frequently made by hand out of knots or simple beads and string, would have been used by charmers of the medieval and early modern periods, representing what writers at the time referred to as "papish" magical traditions among the lower classes of society. It is sometimes claimed that common folk did not understand the Latin prayers used by priests and monks, and so they became garbled and jumbled into "ignorant" forms of incantations; I would like to offer a different interpretation, one that honors the ingenuity of our cunning ancestors. While unschooled in Latin, they perhaps understood the true function of the prayer as incantation better than the priests themselves, improvising with their salt-of-the-earth genius the use of Latinate charms into their own folk craft, in effect claiming and owning the language of the most powerful force of their time (the church) and bending it to serve their own purposes.

Rather than viewing this blended body of practices as ignorant, folk witches today should recognize its genius. It is due to the brilliant improvisation of those charmers of old that we are today able to call upon our Old Ones with the very language of those who sought to stamp them out, a radical act of charming that embodies the resistance at the very heart of our craft. Those wishing to explore the role of the fabled "paternoster" charms of Scottish folk craft will find versions in my previous work, *The Witch's Art of Incantation: Spoken Charms, Spells, and Curses in Folk Witchcraft.*

The magical acts of counting also encompass the variety of spoken charms designed to be used in repetition, such as the waulking and repetitive chore-song incantations recorded in Carmichael's (1900) *Carmina Gadelica*, a collection of folk incantations gathered in Scotland in the late 1800s. Notable charms collected by Carmichael involved in repetitious acts include the following for the shearing of sheep:

> Go shorn and come woolly,
> Bear the Beltane female lamb,
> Be the lovely Bride thee endowing,
> And the fair Mary thee sustaining,
> The fair Mary sustaining thee...

The following incantation is provided as a weaver's charm to be sung or spoken to accompany work on the loom:

> Thrums nor odds of thread
> My hand never kept, nor shall keep,
>
> Every color in the bow of the shower
> Has gone through my fingers beneath the cross,
>
> White and black, red and madder,
> Green, dark grey, and scarlet...

The songs recorded by Carmichael blur the line between prayer, poem, and incantation, revealing the interconnected nature of folk magic and folk religion as understood by our cunning craft ancestors, incorporating both the names of saints and the powers of nature in the form of moon, sun, stars, plants, and animals. The lyrical design of these charms is clearly meant to encompass mnemonic devices for easy recall and repetition of the charmer. Some are most explicit in their emphasis on counting and repetition:

> Well can I say my rune,
> Descending with the glen;
>> One rune,
>> Two runes
>> Three runes,
>> Four runes,
>> Five runes,
>> Six runes,
>> Seven runes,
>> Seven and a half runes...

Here, we should interpret "rune" as "mystery" or "mysterious charm," though it is worth noting that frequent Nordic invasions would have brought elements of northern paganism into the charming practices of the Scots.

The power of the repetitious act to facilitate shifts of consciousness are well-attested in pagan lore and the deities associated with such meticulous aspects of labor. Freya, an ancient Norse goddess, was known as the teacher of *seithr*, a form of magic involving altered consciousness and trance states. It is worth noting that, etymologically, the term *seithr* is connected with early Indo-European terms for "string," "rope," and "binding." In addition to this form of trance-magic, Freya is associated with *galdr* (the performance of memorized songs as a magical act) and the fiber-arts, frequently wielding a distaff used for spinning wool, and is said in some lore to fly across the land by its use. An older folk-term for the constellation called Orion's Belt is actually Freya's Distaff, as recorded in the early 1800s:

> And then the green, green pine trees, that fade never,
> That Odin's thunderbolts alone destroy,
> All these things I do love; for these are Nature,
> That lifts our heavenward gaze to Aukthor's car
> And Freya's distaff, weaving lives of men...
> (Oehlanschlaeger, 1821)

Perhaps it is here we see the ancient connection between the arts of weaving, spinning, braiding, knotting, knitting, tying—virtually all of the fiber arts—and the shift to otherworldly consciousness that the sorcerous among us still seek to this day. Our ancient pagan ancestors observed the effects of repetitive tasks upon their own consciousness, a gate of otherworldly access that remains open to folk witches today.

Committed to memory, the arts grouped under *via repetitio* empower the witch with access to otherworldly power in virtually any setting, the only necessary preparation being understanding and experience in wielding the chosen formula. Though seemingly simple, these necessities—understanding and experience—are hard-won treasures, requiring careful approach and regular practice over time. Beginners should note that the repetitive act, though an excellent facilitator of ecstasy, will not in and of itself yield results. The witch should allow their entire consciousness to focus solely on the repetitive act or utterance, becoming so absorbed in its rhythms that all else ceases to exist. This point of focus, held for a length of time on something outside of the mind's usual thoughts, will eventually give way and allow the practitioner access to this gate of the spirit.

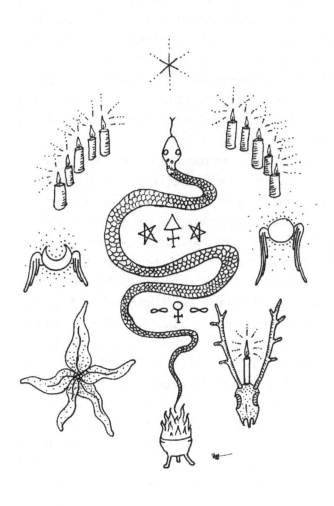

Via Flammae

Fireflies dart and glow over the hills like earth-bound stars. The horizon is still blue-black with the onset of darkness, the moon still low over the land. Working quickly, the witch arranges dried branches for the fire, propping their lengths against each other, preparing them to adequately feed the hunger of the flame that will be set this night. A fire is alive, the witch knows; it needs to breathe and to consume like any living thing.

Tonight, the bonfire is lit for the Old Ones. It begins small, crackling and fizzing through the slight damp in the wood from a recent rain. Then it grows. The flames reach up toward the dark above like so many arms from the otherworld, hungry for air, for breath. The hot ash from the fire's base, rising and coiling into the air, mingles with the glow of the fireflies, casting stars into the shadow.

As the fire begins to find its pace, to accelerate into a steady growth, the witch gazes into the red coals beneath the wood. Here is the seed of fire, raw and ravaging. With a deep breath to gather strength for the work to come, the witch speaks to the fire's embers, brow furrowed, *annunciating clearly so as to be heard by those behind the heat and light therein:*

> *Hail, serpent and lion of the fire.*
> *Hail, water and leaf-thick tree.*
>
> *Hail, self-gendered one,*
> *invisible, fiery begetter of light.*
>
> *Enter into this fire, and fill it.*
> *Let you who dwell within shine through.* [*]

A stir of orange ash rises as a branch falls in the fire. The witch knows that this is a sign of the listener, of the old serpent of art. They slip several more branches into the fire's arrangement of sticks to keep it fed. The fire, the witch knows, is both gate and offering, speculum and fumigant. It is through the fire that the door to the otherworld is opened, and it is through that which is burned that the dread powers there are satisfied.

Sitting before the fire, the witch leans in from a comfortable distance. They feel the blood rush to their cheeks to meet the flame's radiant heat. The red-hot base of the flame, the heart of fire, could almost be a glowing passageway, the mouth of a volcano. Knowing that the mysteries of fire are not for the weak, the witch speaks the

---

[*] This ancient formula is adapted from the *Greek Magical Papyri*, written sometime between 100 B.C.E. and 400 C.E. The influence of the Mithras cult can here be traced, which would eventually color modern images of Lucifer.

gate-crossing charm assertively:

> Open my eyes. Open my eyes.
> Great serpent of the East,
>
> dawn-riser, great craftsman,
> open to me this vessel of flame
>
> upon the primeval waters.
> Speak to me through this mouth,
>
> breathe upon me with this light,
> and open for me the gate I seek.[*]

The witch sits still for a moment, waiting, gazing into the embers. The night has risen around them, and all else but the fire's light is darkness. Subtly at first, the witch feels the pull.

The rhythmic undulations of the flame, the sound of constant crackling, the glow at the base of the fire all serve to focus the witch's eye. All of the witch's attention is bound up in that fire, in its waves and gestures, mysterious and ever-shifting. All else is darkness. The light at the center of the fire seems to brighten somehow, to open somehow, and the witch can feel the spirit loosening within the body, ready to make the journey.

---

[*] Another incantation adapted from the *Greek Magical Papyri*. Serpents and fire featured commonly in the Mithraism of the time, much to the horror of biblical scholars who would later find similarities between the Mithraic rites and the Christian eucharist.

Breathe upon me with this breath,
and open for me the gate...

The witch opens their mouth and exhales slow and long,
releasing the fetch-body to ride upon the deep, circling over
the fire's glow, then descending down into its radiant
depths, deeper and deeper through that white-hot tunnel,
the gate to the otherworld, to those hidden people, and to
the wisdom and power they keep safeguarded for those who
possess the skill to make the journey.

~ 👈 ~

The presence of fire marks both the simple folk ritual and the ornate. It is present as the candle lit upon the altar, the herbs burned to release their air-born properties, the bonfire swelling with light and heat. The history and lore of fire rites in folk craft emphasize fire's properties of destruction and rebirth, of illuminating darkness, and of guiding the practitioner upon hidden paths.

Many folk witches today (though not all) operating within Celtic currents of our art associate fire with the cross-quarter days of May Eve or Beltane, Lammas, All Hallows' Eve, and Candlemas. Frazier (1922) describes the practice of the Beltane fire in northeastern Scotland in the late 1700s:

...the herdsmen of several farms used to gather dry
wood, kindle it, and dance three times 'southways'
about the burning pile. But in this region, according
to a later authority, the Beltane fires were lit not on
the first but on the second of May, Old Style. They
were called bone-fires. The people believed that on
that evening and night the witches were abroad and
busy casting spells on cattle and stealing cows' milk.

This fire was in many ways intended to deter dark
spirits and the workings of malevolent witches, but
as is often the case in folk craft, the apparent
intention of this work belies a deeper significance.
The presence of the bonfire on these specific
occasions, most frequently those cross-quarter
days, connects this custom with the trooping or
traveling fae, who moved about the land on these
nights, as described by Kirk in 1691. Moreover,
Frazier's research reveals the presence of offerings
in the fire: specific kinds of wood burned to
propitiate spirits, cakes made of oatmeal, butter,
and other easily prepared dishes, all cast into the
yawning mouth of the flame on these nights. This
complicates the portrayal of these fires as merely
protective, suggesting instead a historical
connection between the fire and the passageways
by which the denizens of the otherworld travel
about the land on certain nights of the year. The
fact that some of the folk customs described by
Frazier include observants themselves eating

portions of the offerings cast in the fire suggests a kind of spiritual communion, a sharing of nourishment between the worlds.

The famous image of the Jack-o'-lantern carved and lit on All Hallows' Eve is of course a residual of these ancient fire customs made popular in North America largely by the influence of Irish immigrants. Allies (1852) described the use of the term "Hob and his Lantern" in Worcestershire, and connects the various terms for this lantern ritual:

> ...they are called by the names of "Hoberdy's Lantern," "Hobany's Lantern," "Hob and his Lantern," "Jack-o'-Lantern," and "Will-o'-the-Wisp."

Here, we see that the old appellation of the Devil as "Old Hob" present in this preserved lore of this ritual and the connection to the Will-o'-Wisp, otherwise described in our lore as a luminous apparition that appears frequently around ancient sacrificial bogs and prehistoric burial sites.

This connection between naming conventions for the same lantern ritual emphasizes the light within the lantern as one actually lit in the Devil's name, that Devil being emblematic of the first sorcerers, those old shamanic practitioners of our past, dead and buried, in their horned headdresses and animal garb designed to mimic the creatures of the hunt. It is to that Old One that the

Jack-o'-Lantern is lit, and to the memory of those first charmers, preserved in the words and symbols of this ancient rite. Despite the popularization of the Jack-o'-Lantern as a tradition devoid of any spiritual substance, many folk witches today honor the Old Hob with the lighting of a carved squash or turnip, set upon the porch of the house as a kind of totemic offering.

The folk witch's charm-work of going forth as "witch-fire" is recorded in our lore, connecting the will-o'-wisp with the witch himself. Davis' (1975) collection of American colonial witch-lore titled *The Silver Bullet* recounts the following description of a witch going forth as fire:

> After a long, hard night of chasing raccoons and trudging over hills and valleys, the hunters came upon a fence and sat down to rest before climbing it. Suddenly, a blazing reddish-yellow ball of fire appeared in front of them. It skidded to and fro aimlessly, then lodged on a nearby tree trunk. Its color faded to a pale blue and it gradually assumed a human form. The phantom thrashed and squirmed about like an entrapped animal trying to free itself. This terrifying apparition froze the hunters motionless. Finally, the youngest boy managed to get to his feet and shoot at the phantom. It vanished like a streak of lightning.

The witch in Davis' tale is later found at the hunters' home, gazing into the fire while stirring an herbal preparation to treat a sick relative. Tales like this one reveal the overlapping folkloric belief in witches' flights and the cunning craft of herb-doctors in the Appalachian mountains, those charms and folk-magical practices carried over from the old world to the new.

Further, we see that the ritual use of light itself bears a strong folkloric connection to the Devil of our sabbat, as described in the folkloric work of Thompson (1929):

> Candles (or torches) also figure prominently in pre-Christian Candlemas festivals and were sometimes carried by the devil, as a true Lucifer, upon his head; while the phrase 'to hold a candle to the devil,' that is while he performed various rites, has become a common expression.

Thompson's use of the term "true Lucifer" here is arresting in its referral to the Devil as light-bearer. We see this connection in the biblical Isaiah's phrasing of "O Lucifer, son of the morning," but also in the mythology of the ancient world, since Romans used the term to describe the planet Venus in its appearance as the morning star.

These images of horned figures with light between their antlers or horns are pervasive in the folkloric landscape of old craft, even surviving the shifting tides of religion. According to Thompson, even the saints of Christianity, in order to increase the spread of their tales and the faith itself across

Western Europe, adopted elements of the sabbatic goat with his light between the horns:

> One meets forlorn chapels to St. Leonard on heaths and lonely places; and 'Leonard' in the *Pseudomonarchia Daemonium* of Wierus, was one of the four great princes of hell, black master of the Sabbath and inspector-general of magic and sorcery. St. Hubert's conversion was effected, while he was hunting on Good Friday, by a miraculous stag which bore a crucifix or cross surrounded by rays of light between its horns. Thus he became the patron saint of hunters, with his feast day on November 3rd...

Today, witches continue to be divided on the topic of Lucifer as ancestor/deity, but those who recognize this Old One in their craft honor him not as a tempter or punisher in line with the Satan of the bible, but as a teacher and illuminator of mysteries as he appears in Leland's (1899) *Aradia: Gospel of the Witches.* Even the pentagram itself, which has been adopted as a symbol of modern witchcraft as a whole, is made up of five lines tracing the movement of the planet Venus (the morning star) in relation to the earth.

Just as the flame in folk and traditional witchcraft suggests an illumination of mysteries and a living embodiment of the spirits of the otherworld, so too does it offer a window through which the witch's spirit may pass. The ancient art of pyromancy, being divination by fire and the trance states induced thereof, reinforces fire's agency as a connective point between the worlds. Agrippa (1533) described various customs of pyromancy in his influential *Three Books of Occult Philosophy*:

> ...Pyromancy divines by fiery impressions, and by stars with long tails, by fiery colors, by visions and imaginations in the fire. So the wife of Cicero foretold that he would be consul the next year because, when a certain man, after the sacrifice was ended, would look in the ashes, there suddenly broke forth a flame. Of this kind are those that Pliny speaks of—that terrene, pale and buzzing fires presage tempests, circles about the snuffs of candles betoken rain, and if the flame fly, turning and winding, it portends wind. Also torches, when they strike the fire before them and are not kindled. Also when a coal sticks to a pot taken off from the fire, and when the fire casts off the ashes and sparkles; or when ashes are hard grown together on the hearth, and when a coal is very bright.

The ancients understood as well as we do that the act of gazing into a fire for extended periods of time induces a powerful hypnotic effect, and modern practitioners use a flame as simple as a small candle to facilitate the shift in consciousness necessary for potent spirit work. A key element to the mastery of this art, however, lies in the contrast between light and darkness in the ritual space, whether outdoors or indoors. Ideally, the flame utilized in spirit flight should be the sole source of light in the chosen space. In the absence of other lights, the isolated flame becomes a focused point of brilliance that, with practice and concentration, gives way to a luminous tunnel to the otherworld by way of witch-sight.

Via Umbrum

Upon the darkest night of the year, the witch steels herself with whiskey, its sweet burn bracing her heart for the challenge that is to come. This is a night for courage, for grit. This is a night for calling to the shadow by name, for facing the enemy within, for tearing down what is weak and ill-made in order to rebuild, to fortify the spirit with mettle. This is a night to step into true power, to become strong.

The witch needs no tools this night, no ingredients, no preparations. The charm is simple and true, its goals and means older than much of her art. Tonight, she will call upon those dread powers in the abyss and open the Black Book. She will gaze into its visions for wisdom and charms preserved in the space between worlds. In her working space, perfectly dark but for a single candle, the witch speaks soulfully:

Ye dread powers of the night,

ye Old Ones of the groves, [*]
I deliver myself willingly
unto your perfect darkness.

*She focuses herself now, seeing clearly the church in which
she was raised, witnessing the image of her own baptism,
that moment at which her soul was promised to an ancient
being she never wished to serve. She will belong to herself
now, and herself alone. Ready to sever the bond, she speaks
the words:*

*Three times do I deny the claim upon my soul.
I deny the oppressor who would rule me.
I deny the fear that would restrain me.
I deny the false friend who would keep me.* [†]

*Crouching upon the ground, the witch places one hand over
her head and another beneath the sole of her left foot, the
whole of her held between her two hands, herself holding
herself, a sign of ownership over her entire being.*

Eman Hetan, O Eman Hetan, [‡]
*From the top of my head
to the soles of my feet,*

---

[*] These first two lines echo the language in the poet Ovid's ancient prayer to the powers of night itself.

[†] To thrice deny one's allegiance to the Christian god is a common motif recorded in early modern witch-lore.

[‡] The appellation "Eman Hetan" is of unknown origin, though likely Basque. It appears in a description of a witches' chant in Ainsworth's *Crichton* in 1837.

I hold myself within myself.
Like you, I claim myself for myself,
and in so doing, become of thee.

The witch rises, closing her eyes, focusing her witch-sight.
Somewhere in the room, somewhere in that darkness,
another set of eyes gaze upon her. A shadow stirs. She feels
the breath of that Old One stirring the air in the room. She
feels him stand behind her, not as a predator come to seek
its prey, but as a teacher witnessing a student meet the
measure of the lesson, approving. As a shadow hand is
placed upon her shoulder, she feels a shift in the atmosphere,
like a cloud releasing its waters or a vacuum coming
unsealed. The darkness all around her is full of paths now,
paths she might take to various worlds and lessons, paths to
the hidden arcana of the shadow, paths of the spirit. Freed
of her bonds and ready to make the journey, the witch speaks
the old words of the charm:

Open for me the Black Book of Art
that I may gaze into its secrets dark.
Obymero per noctem et Symeam
et membres membris
*et Lasys cawtis nomis et Arypys.**

~ 🖎 ~

---

* The garbled Latin formula here is adapted from the 16th century
grimoire titled *The Book of Magic*, Folger Shakespeare Library MS. V.b.26.

Although many early modern accounts from witch-hunters describe the supposed "Devil's baptism," there are few trial records mentioning it at all. In Scotland, there are nearly none (Murray, 1921). Instead, the Devil appears to the witch in one or a variety of spiritual forms that can be at times frightful:

> At Angers in 1593, the Black Man transformed himself first into a goat and then into a young bull; in Guernsey in 1563 he was a large black cat who led the dance; in 1616 at Brecy he was a black dog who stood on his hind-legs and preached; at Poictiers in 1574 he was a goat who talked like a person; at Avignon in 1581, when he mounted on an alter to be adored 'he instantly turns himself into the form of a great black goat, although on all other occasions he useth to appear in the shape of a man.' In Auldearne in 1662 'sometimes he would be like a stirk, a bull, a deer, a roe, or a dog.' (Murray, 1931)

Most frequently in surviving lore, the Devil or Man in Black then asks the witch to form some manner of agreement, often involving the renunciation of baptismal vows, and permits the witch access to the fabled Black Book of Art. In MacKenzie's 1699 account, the Devil places his hand on the head of the supplicant, then asks for ownership over everything under his hand; in Isobel Gowdie's testimony from the same century, she describes how the Devil "did put the on of my handis to the crowne of my head and the uther to the sole of my foote and then reununcent all betuxt my two handis over to the Divell" (Howard, 2013). These diabolical elements of our lore have largely been shrugged off by New Age practitioners, but there is a seed of wisdom here preserved for the wise.

It is easy, in modern witchcraft, to wince at the more subversive practices preserved in the treasures of our lore: the deal made at the crossroads, the trampling of the cross, the renunciation of baptism. Many magical practitioners today refer to themselves as "light-workers," and to be certain, it is easy to look only towards "the light," focusing instead on what we consider (by whatever simplistic and flawed measure) to be purely benevolent deities, putting all of our efforts into healing work, blessing charms, forever sweeping the darkness from our view. We have been taught, after all, that dark things are dangerous, and that the light is by its very nature benevolent.

We are afraid to gaze into the dark. We are afraid of what we might find there, of what we have been told is waiting there. And so we sweep the Devil of our craft under the rug. And so we gaze increasingly into the light, into that hallowed, cleansing, purifying, cauterizing source of light— until it leaves us burned and blind. And then we wonder why the salt is missing from the meal, why the flavor has gone, why the potency can't be felt, why we cannot see or hear our teachers beside us in the dark.

A large part of the false antagonism between light and dark in modern magical discourse can be explained as a misinterpretation of the left-right dichotomy in Western esotericism. The term "right-hand path" has been used to refer to spiritual traditions that seek the dissolution of the egoistic self into a larger whole. This term has been applied to paths with a goal of enlightenment, salvation, or a path to heaven, where the old egoistic self is shed in order to join that bright and unifying light. "Left-hand path," according to esotericists, describes traditions that seek the preservation and empowerment of the individual self, the desire for personal fulfillment and individuation rather than communion with the greater whole. This term has been used to describe Satanists and others who place more value on individual freedom.

While esotericists debate and pontificate over the intricacies of these two models, folk craft offers a simpler view, one grounded in traditions of magical practice that still live to this day. My cunning craft ancestors did not subscribe to any such "left-right" model of practice. They healed and blessed frequently, and they cursed those who would harm their loved ones. What's more, they performed these charms drawing on surviving pagan tradition alongside a folk version of what the church offered. Even a cursory glance at this passage from Psalm 69, a famous cursing psalm used by folk witches to this day, confounds the idea that the Bible itself offers a completely benevolent, egoless spirituality:

> Let their table become a snare before them: and that which should have been for their welfare, let it become a trap.
>
> Let their eyes be darkened, that they see not; and make their loins continually to shake.
>
> Pour out thine indignation upon them, and let thy wrathful anger take hold of them.
>
> Let their habitation be desolate; and let none dwell in their tents.
>
> For they persecute him whom thou has smitten; and they talk to the grief of those whom thou hast wounded.
>
> Add iniquity unto their iniquity: and let them not come into thy righteousness.
>
> Let them be blotted out of the book of the living, and not be written with the righteous.

While some would say that the desires expressed here do not represent modern-day Christianity, the actions of those who call themselves Christian today would contradict the statement. In truth, all spiritual paths contain both "left" and "right-hand" elements because it is human to desire both personal preservation and the good of one's community. Both perspectives are necessary in any healthy individual.

Darkness, as a spiritual metaphor in modern practice, refers not to evil or malevolence, but to powers that permit withdrawal, restoration, and access to mysterious knowledge. Owls, moths, spiders, bats, and many other helpful creatures rely on darkness in order to feed themselves. Humans rely on darkness in order to rest and dream, our first point of access to the voices of the otherworld, one built into the natural cycles of the body. A world without darkness would be maddening and destructive to us and all other forms of life that we know.

We can approach the work of spirit flight *via umbrum* through the exploration of personal fears, deviation, taboo, and the unknown. In cultures marked by Christianity, calling out to the Devil creates an emotional tension within the practitioner, a friction of the deviant self acting against the dominant culture, and this tension can be fruitful for experiencing ecstatic states. Similarly, confronting personal fears can create this state in the practitioner. Darkness facilitates this process because it allows the mind to drown out stimuli and experience wonder (and sometimes terror) in the face of the unknown.

The craft of experiencing otherworldly stimuli by stepping into the unknown is preserved in many folk charms, even outside of the traditional rite of the midnight visit to the crossroads, including the Scottish frith and casting of the clew and the Swedish Arsgang (or "year walk"). In the frith, a spoken charm is performed upon the intended party, who then steps through a door and departs on a walk that will reveal hidden meanings. All things seen and experienced on this walk are considered messages from the otherworld, but the first thing seen is particularly significant. Carmichael (1900) gives a Christianized version of this spoken charm, though its inclusion of the pagan goddess Brigit as Mary's midwife or maid reveals its more ancient roots:

> The augury that Mary made for her Son,
> That Brigit breathed through her palm;
> Hast thou seen the augury, guiding maid?
> The young maid said that she had.
>
> Message of truth without message of falsehood,
> That I myself may see
> The semblance, joyous and mild,
> Of all that is amissing to me.

This is similar to the Swedish year walk, which is also a divinatory event, interpreting things seen and experienced while walking as messages from the otherworld. The casting of the clew, which is associated strongly with All Hallows' Eve and has been described as a rite of the Scottish Nicneven or the Gyre Carlin, involves throwing a ball of string or yarn into some dark area, originally an old kiln. As the thread is drawn back through the witch's hands, she speaks to the darkness, asking who holds the other end.

Preserved in the symbolism of the crossroads itself is the intersection between planes and forms of consciousness. The very symbol of the six seasonal festivals on which the Good People are said to travel about the land converts to a three-dimensional model, rendering by its three lines the geometrical figure of the cube, defining a single point of focus by six outward points. It is worth noting here that this crossroads sigil is also the letter *eabhadh* of the forfeda (five letters of later addition to the ogham), which represents the salmon of knowledge, originally a serpent (noted among folklorists as Aarne-Thompson 673, a motif sometimes referred to as "The White Serpent's Flesh"). In this folkloric motif, the flesh of a serpent or fish is eaten in order to gain wisdom, much similar to the serpent offering fruit in the story of the Garden of Eden. Witches would do well to meditate on the forms and computations of this three-lined glyph, for this symbol of the crossroads speaks at once to formations of time, space, and the overlapping of forms of consciousness in the achievement of sabbatic ekstasis. Its figure renders a glimpse at the geometry of the dark and unknown that we hold sacred.

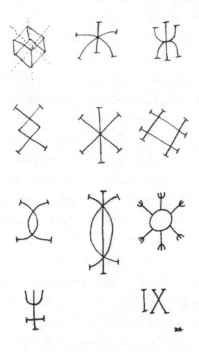

Even the simple act of speaking to an unseen other in the darkness holds massive potency for modern witches. In an age in which we can buy prepared herbs and astrological almanacs, we have grown unaccustomed to the shadow. We balk at the idea of being forced to summon actual courage for our craft. More than anything, perhaps, witches are afraid of finding the darkness on the periphery experience to be a reflection of the darkness that is part of our nature, our inheritance.

Perhaps the ultimate folkloric source of fear and horror in the dark is Hell itself. Witches, being threatened by Christians with the prospect of Hell to this day, would do well to meditate upon the mysteries preserved in stories of Hell, to dissect its actual lore-born components. Thomas the Rhymer gives a 1300s picture of the folk belief in the "tithe to Hell," which the denizens of Elphame were required to pay every seven years in the form of a human captive soul. Elphame or Elfland is frequently described in the lore of the time as lying on the outskirts of Hell itself. People able to travel to and from this kingdom unwounded in the lore tend to be sorcerous characters, witches and charmers. The name "Hell" itself comes, of course, from Hel, Norse goddess and queen of Niflheim, the World of Darkness and the kingdom of the dead. Rather than being a place of punishment, the innocent dead were described as being treated kindly by Hel at her banquet table (Guerber, 1995). Her face was said to be half beautiful and half corpse-like.

In the half-living, half-dead image of Hell's queen, we see an echo of our own nature as creatures straddling two worlds. Does the two-natured form of this dark queen–this "regina pigmeorum," to quote the language of William Lilly when describing the Queen of Elphame in the mid-1600s–not echo the doubled nature of the Devil of our lore? While she is half living and half-dead, he is half man and half animal. What does the two-fold natures of these Old Ones have to teach us as voyagers upon the otherworld's deep? What wisdom is preserved in their two-bodied natures? What are we witches living and practicing today if not echoes of their own peculiar mysteries, their own endlessly unfolding darkness?

Ritual Appendix

The following outlines offer simplified, easy-reference versions of the methods discussed and described in this work. Although these short-hand ritual instructions have proven themselves effective, folk witchcraft is ever a flexible, personalized practice. Certain elements of each rite are at the discretion of the witch (the call to the Old Ones, altar arrangements, etc.), while others are specific to the charm. Adaptation, rearrangement, and revision are not only acceptable, but traditional; individual witches have always adapted their personal versions of charms based on their own experimentation. It is recommended that individual witches explore the folklore of their ancestry and their land and incorporate the guidance of their familiar spirits in the development of a personal repertoire of charm and art.

A Stang or Besom Rite
(Via Equarum)

I.   Gather your broom, staff, or stang, and
        arrange your altar. If you do not yet have
        your own approach to altar work, I
        recommend a pleasing arrangement of
        flora (dried flowers, leaves, or branches to
        represent the Lady or Queen of Elphame)
        and fauna (bones, teeth, etc., to represent
        the Devil or King of Elphame) as well as a
        central candle.

II.   Begin by breathing deeply and relaxing
        your body. Quiet your bodily senses, and
        awaken your witch-sight. Consult pp. 53-55
        for instructions on this step if needed.

III.   If desired, consecrate the space between
        the worlds using the crossroads charm
        from p. 66 or the ring of art charm from p.
        147.

IV.   Call to the Old Ones of your ancestry and
        your craft in what way seems best to you.
        If you do not yet have a formula of your

232 Roger J. Horne

own, consider using the one on p. 73.

V. Sitting comfortably on the floor, grip your besom, staff, or stang with the solid end upon the floor in front of you. Lean your weight slightly upon it. Feel it bearing the weight of your body.

VI. Slowly, with intention, repeat the following (or the charm of your choice), calling your familiar spirit into the vessel of broom, stang, or staff:

> *Famulus, I conjure you.*
> *[Name], my faithful familiar,*
> *I conjure your spirit into this vessel*
> *of wood and art*
> *that you might convey me to the otherworld*
> *thither by night, by air, and by the dark.*

VII. Allow your familiar to pull your spirit form with it as it embarks with these words, chanted repeatedly:

> *Horse and hattock.*
> *Horse and go.*
> *Horse and pellatis.*
> *Ho, ho.*

A Tree Rite
(Via Arborum)

I.   Select a tree on or near your dwelling, and
      offer it water. Identify its species, and
      learn some of the lore of its nature. Ask
      for a leaf, twig, or bud to take with you
      using the following charm:

      Mother, give me some of thee,
      and when I am become a tree,
      I shall give thee some of me.
      For I am of thee, and thou art mine,
      and I have nothing which is not thine.

II.   Commit the form of the tree to memory.
      Spend some time gazing upon it carefully.
      Notice its branches, visible roots, and
      bark. Look carefully for a crevice or
      opening.

III. Gather the bit taken from the tree, and
      arrange your altar. If you do not yet have
      your own approach to altar work, I

recommend a pleasing arrangement of flora (dried flowers, leaves, or branches to represent the Lady or Queen of Elphame) and fauna (bones, teeth, etc., to represent the Devil or King of Elphame) as well as a central candle.

IV.   Begin by breathing deeply and relaxing your body. Quiet your bodily senses, and awaken your witch-sight. Consult pp. 53-55 for instructions on this step if needed.

V.   If desired, consecrate the space between the worlds using the crossroads charm from p. 66 or the ring of art charm from pp. 147.

VI.   Call to the Old Ones of your ancestry and your craft in what way seems best to you. If you do not yet have a formula of your own, consider using the one on p. 73.

VII.   Holding the leaf or twig, focus your witch-sight on the tree's form and its crevice or opening. Speak the following (or a charm of your own):

Here do I speak a sain of going.
Sain of seven paters, one.
Sain of seven paters, two.
Sain of seven paters, three.
Sain of seven paters, four.
Sain of seven paters, five.
Sain of seven paters, six.

Sain of seven paters, seven.

VIII.   Move your spirit through the crevice of
the tree, and allow its branches to become
tunneling hallways. Choose a path.

A Holed Stone Rite
(Via Lapidum)

I. Gather a holed stone, and arrange your
    altar. If you do not yet have your own
    approach to altar work, I recommend a
    pleasing arrangement of flora (dried
    flowers, leaves, or branches to represent
    the Lady or Queen of Elphame) and fauna
    (bones, teeth, etc., to represent the Devil
    or King of Elphame) as well as a central
    candle.

II. Begin by breathing deeply and relaxing
     your body. Quiet your bodily senses, and
     awaken your witch-sight. Consult pp. 53-55
     for instructions on this step if needed.

III. If desired, consecrate the space between
     the worlds using the crossroads charm
     from p. 66 or the ring of art charm from p.
     147.

IV. Call to the Old Ones of your ancestry and
     your craft in what way seems best to you.
     If you do not yet have a formula of your

own, consider using the one on p. 73.

V.   Holding the stone intently in your hand, speak the following charm (or one of your own choosing), feeling the stone awaken as you do so:

I conjure you, O adder stone
tunneled by the serpent's body.

I conjure you, O hag stone,
bore through even as the caves of the earth
and the rushing streams upon it.

I conjure you, O holey stone,
through which the Old Ones pass.

Hal, hal, aoirinn,
hiu bhidil hiu bhi
hal, hal, aoirinn,
Puca Geal, Puca Dubh.

VI.   Focus upon the sensations of the stone in your hand, and allow your witch-sight to perceive the sensation of your hands along the cool, stony entrance of a cave. Step through.

A Rite of the Grave
(Via Mortuorum)

I.   Make an offering of bread or wine to the
       spirits of a local churchyard, then gather
       graveyard dirt in kindness and gratitude.

II.   At home, arrange your altar. Be sure to
       have some form of incense or herbal
       fumigation. If you do not yet have your
       own approach to altar work, I recommend
       a pleasing arrangement of flora (dried
       flowers, leaves, or branches to represent
       the Lady or Queen of Elphame) and fauna
       (bones, teeth, etc., to represent the Devil
       or King of Elphame) as well as a central
       candle.

III.   Begin by breathing deeply and relaxing
       your body. Quiet your bodily senses, and
       awaken your witch-sight. Consult pp. 53-55
       for instructions on this step if needed.

IV.   If desired, consecrate the space between
       the worlds using the crossroads charm
       from p. 66 or the ring of art charm from p.

147.

V. Call to the Old Ones of your ancestry and your craft in what way seems best to you. If you do not yet have a formula of your own, consider using the one on p. 73.

VI. Hold the graveyard dirt in your dominant hand. Feel out the potency in the particles of bone and flesh present in the soil. Hold it over the lit fumigation, allowing the smoke to perfume the bottle in your hand, speaking the following or a charm of your own choosing:

Honored ones, from your graves, I call you.
With prayer and fumigation, I call you.
With bone and leaf, I call you.
With love and offering, I call you.

Teh Beh Ripahr
Ichi Pass
Ez Peh Lah Tem
Ex Wah Yameh
Queh Warren
Peh Riesh The

VII. Allowing part or all of the words above to become a repeated chant, feel the presence of the dead about you. Allow them to rise from the shadows of the room to meet the welcome of the charm. When you feel prepared, knock three times upon the floor to open the gate through which your spirit may pass.

An Anointing Rite
(Via Veneficium)

I.   Concoct a simple oil or unguent from a plant conducive to transvection. A very safe oil can be made from steeping one part dried mugwort in two parts sweet almond oil, sealed in a jar and left in the warmth of the sun for at least three weeks, then strained. Be wary of working with nightshades. If you lack experience in this area, consider buying one prepared by a knowledgeable and trustworthy herbalist.

II. Collect your oil, and arrange your altar. If you do not yet have your own approach to altar work, I recommend a pleasing arrangement of flora (dried flowers, leaves, or branches to represent the Lady or Queen of Elphame) and fauna (bones, teeth, etc., to represent the Devil or King of Elphame) as well as a central candle.

III. Begin by breathing deeply and relaxing your body. Quiet your bodily senses, and awaken your witch-sight. Consult pp. 53-55 for instructions on this step if needed.

IV. If desired, consecrate the space between the worlds using the crossroads charm from p. 66 or the ring of art charm from p. 147

V. Call to the Old Ones of your ancestry and your craft in what way seems best to you. If you do not yet have a formula of your own, consider using the one on p. 73.

VI. As you anoint yourself with the oil, massaging it well into the skin, repeat the following incantation or one of your own choosing:

Bazabi lacha bachabe
Lamach cahi achabahe
   Karrelyos
Lamach Lamech Bachalyos
Cabahagy Sabalyos
   Baryolas
Lagoz atha Cabyolas
Samatha atha Famolas
   Hurrahya
   Hurrahya
   Hurrahya

VII. Feel the oil sink into the body and into the spirit, loosening it from the grip of skin. Take your time to allow the oil's effects to manifest. When you are ready to embark, allow your spirit to move over your teeth and between your lips with a long exhalation.

A Dream Rite
(Via Somnium)

I.   Gather a small amount of oil with a pleasing scent or dream-inducing properties. Consider using the mugwort oil in the via veneficium appendix or craft one of your own. Lavender is lovely.

II.   On an evening before going to bed, begin by breathing deeply and relaxing your body. Quiet your bodily senses, and awaken your witch-sight. Consult pp. 53-55 for instructions on this step if needed.

III. If desired, consecrate the space between the worlds using the crossroads charm from p. 66 or the ring of art charm from p. 147

IV.   Call to the Old Ones of your ancestry and your craft in what way seems best to you. If you do not yet have a formula of your own, consider using the one on p. 73.

V.   Anoint yourself with the oil, and with a trace of it on your finger, make three crosses upon the bed where you will rest, repeating this charm or one of your choosing:

In the days when the Old Ones walked,
our queen's beloved lay cursed in his bed,
and so she called in the moonlight
to charm a place out of their dreaming.
Three crosses on his bed she made
to fix the gate to the sabbat-realm
so that the unwise could not enter
and no power of sleep or death
could part them. So do I draw open
the gates of the dreaming sabbat
to dwell for a time in that fair land.

VI.   Before sleeping, blow gently upon the spot on the bed where you signed three crosses. Feel your breath open the barrier, bending the spirit world in that spot. Speak the charm:

Old Ones, guard me on the path tonight
that I might safely cross the threshold
and return once more, by and by.

A Water and Cauldron Rite
(Via Aquum)

I.   Gather a small cauldron or cast iron pot
        and a vessel of fresh water. Arrange your
        altar. If you do not yet have your own
        approach to altar work, I recommend a
        pleasing arrangement of flora (dried
        flowers, leaves, or branches to represent
        the Lady or Queen of Elphame) and fauna
        (bones, teeth, etc., to represent the Devil
        or King of Elphame) as well as a central
        candle.

II.   Begin by breathing deeply and relaxing
        your body. Quiet your bodily senses, and
        awaken your witch-sight. Consult pp. 53-55
        for instructions on this step if needed.

III.   If desired, consecrate the space between
        the worlds using the crossroads charm
        from p. 66 or the ring of art charm from p.
        147.

IV.   Call to the Old Ones of your ancestry and
        your craft in what way seems best to you.

If you do not yet have a formula of your own, consider using the one on p. 73.

V.   As you pour the water into the cauldron, speak these or similar words of your choosing:

> *Old Ones, grant me passage here*
> *for I am of thee, and thou art mine,*
> *and I have nothing which is not thine.*

VI.   Gaze upon the still blackness of the water until you perceive its endless depth, its door of passage between the worlds. When you are ready, speak the words:

> *Descendat spiritus*
> *in hoc speculum.*

Allow your spirit to loosen and depart into the bottomless vessel, beyond the black pool's surface.

A Shapeshifting Rite
(Via Bestium)

I. Gather a bit of hair, bone, tooth, or some other part of an animal of your choice. Use only ethical sources. Those scavenged harmlessly from your own lands are best.

II. Arrange your altar. If you do not yet have your own approach to altar work, I recommend a pleasing arrangement of flora (dried flowers, leaves, or branches to represent the Lady or Queen of Elphame) and fauna (bones, teeth, etc., to represent the Devil or King of Elphame) as well as a central candle.

III. Begin by breathing deeply and relaxing your body. Quiet your bodily senses, and awaken your witch-sight. Consult pp. 53-55 for instructions on this step if needed.

IV. If desired, consecrate the space between the worlds using the crossroads charm from p. 66 or the ring of art charm from p. 147.

V.   Call to the Old Ones of your ancestry and your craft in what way seems best to you. If you do not yet have a formula of your own, consider using the one on p. 73.

VI.   Hold and intentionally feel the animal remains in your hands. Notice its details. Feel the purr of vital energy remaining within it. See the spirit body of the creature that formed it. When you are ready, use the words:

> *Into the shape of a ____ I go*
> *with blackest shout and blackest throw,*
> *and I shall go in Our Lady's name*
> *until I come home again.*

VII.   Slowly, as you repeat the chant, allow your fetch to mimic the creature's form. Refer to pp. 55-57 if you need a refresher on fetch work. Focus on one detail at a time. When you are ready, depart from your body in this bestial form.

A Cartomantic Rite
(Via Imaginibus)

I.   Gather a deck of Marseille tarot cards, and
       arrange your altar. If you do not yet have
       your own approach to altar work, I
       recommend a pleasing arrangement of
       flora (dried flowers, leaves, or branches to
       represent the Lady or Queen of Elphame)
       and fauna (bones, teeth, etc., to represent
       the Devil or King of Elphame) as well as a
       central candle.

II.   Begin by breathing deeply and relaxing
       your body. Quiet your bodily senses, and
       awaken your witch-sight. Consult pp. 53-55
       for instructions on this step if needed.

III.   If desired, consecrate the space between
       the worlds using the crossroads charm
       from p. 66 or the ring of art charm from p.
       147.

IV.   Call to the Old Ones of your ancestry and
       your craft in what way seems best to you.
       If you do not yet have a formula of your

own, consider using the one on p. 73.

V.   From your tarot deck, remove The Devil,
The Moon, The Fool, and The World. As
you set each of the four upon a table's
surface, edge to edge, forming a diamond-
shaped gap between them where all four
edges meet, recite the following:

As the witches of old did call you,
so, too, do I call you, Devil of Art.
I offer you this candle and this incense.

And thou, bright Moon,
first mother of our craft,
come to light the path.

Wandering wild one, child of Cain, come.

And thou, Fortuna, who moves The World
as a wandering globe beneath your feet,
come, come, come.

I conjure not four cards, but four keepers,
four locksmiths, four stewards, four powers
to open the gate between the worlds.

VI.   Place your two hands on either side of the
cartomantic arrangement, and focus on
the diamond-shaped gap between the
cards. Allow it to deepen and swell until it

becomes a gateway. When you are ready, move your spirit through it.

A Wind Rite
(Via Tempestatis)

I.   During a particularly strong storm, step outside. Feel its vibrations in your body. Smell the air. Feel the rain on your skin. Preserve these sensations in your body for later use, committing details to memory.

II.   Store the power of the storm in a knotted cord by feeling its energy in your body, then moving it through your hands as you tie a series of knots. Consider using these words to conjure the storm's power to you as you store the force of the gale:

Boreas, where art thou? Come.
Eurus, where art thou? Come.
Notus, where art thou? Come.
Zephyrus, where art thou? Come.
Bind these winds into such knots of art
that I might use in my craft.

III. When you have need of the transvective

properties of the stored wind, gather the
knotted cord, and arrange your altar. If
you do not yet have your own approach to
altar work, I recommend a pleasing
arrangement of flora (dried flowers,
leaves, or branches to represent the Lady
or Queen of Elphame) and fauna (bones,
teeth, etc., to represent the Devil or King
of Elphame) as well as a central candle.

IV.   Begin by breathing deeply and relaxing
your body. Quiet your bodily senses, and
awaken your witch-sight. Consult pp. 53-55
for instructions on this step if needed.

V.   If desired, consecrate the space between
the worlds using the crossroads charm
from p. 66 or the ring of art charm from p.
147.

VI.   Call to the Old Ones of your ancestry and
your craft in what way seems best to you.
If you do not yet have a formula of your
own, consider using the one on p. 73.

VII.   Feel the force alive in the knotted cord,
and slowly begin to untie one. Feel the
wind of that day beating against you,
pushing your spirit. Open as many knots as
you need to muster the storm power to
carry your spirit from your body.

A Rhythmic Rite
(Via Repetitio)

I. Procure a rosary, but replace the crucifix
    on the end of it with a talisman
    representing an Old One of your ancestry.
    Some options to consider: a bit or horn or
    antler, vertebra of a serpent, dried plant
    matter preserved in a vial, a knot of black
    horse hair. A simpler option is a length of
    string or cord tied with a series of knots.

II. Gather the beads or cord, and arrange
    your altar. If you do not yet have your own
    approach to altar work, I recommend a
    pleasing arrangement of flora (dried
    flowers, leaves, or branches to represent
    the Lady or Queen of Elphame) and fauna
    (bones, teeth, etc., to represent the Devil
    or King of Elphame) as well as a central
    candle.

III. Begin by breathing deeply and relaxing
     your body. Quiet your bodily senses, and
     awaken your witch-sight. Consult pp. 53-55

for instructions on this step if needed.

IV.   If desired, consecrate the space between
the worlds using the crossroads charm
from p. 66 or the ring of art charm from p.
147.

V.   Call to the Old Ones of your ancestry and
your craft in what way seems best to you.
If you do not yet have a formula of your
own, consider using the one on p. 73.

VI.   When you are ready, begin repeating the
chant with each bead counted on the
length. Speak slowly and intentionally, and
allow your mind to open with the
repetitive rhythms of the chant.

I rode a gray horse.
It is called a gray mare.
Gray mane, gray tail,
gray stripe down its back
and not a hair on it
that was not coal-black.

VII.   When the repetition lulls you into a state
of altered consciousness, allow yourself to
perceive a door in the darkness of that
abyss. Knock, and wait for the door to
open.

A Fire Rite
(Via Flammae)

I.   Decide whether to perform your fire rite indoors or outdoors. Both are valid. A candle's flame will work just as well as a raging bonfire.

II.   Light the flame, and arrange your altar. If you do not yet have your own approach to altar work, I recommend a pleasing arrangement of flora (dried flowers, leaves, or branches to represent the Lady or Queen of Elphame) and fauna (bones, teeth, etc., to represent the Devil or King of Elphame) as well as a central candle.

III.   Begin by breathing deeply and relaxing your body. Quiet your bodily senses, and awaken your witch-sight. Consult pp. 53-55 for instructions on this step if needed.

IV.   If desired, consecrate the space between the worlds using the crossroads charm from p. 66 or the ring of art charm from p. 147.

V.   Call to the Old Ones of your ancestry and
      your craft in what way seems best to you.
      If you do not yet have a formula of your
      own, consider using the one on p. 73.
VI.   Gaze into the fire's heart. Speak slowly
      and intentionally into the hottest part of
      the flame in order to be heard:

> *Hail, serpent and lion of the fire.*
> *Hail, water and leaf-thick tree.*
>
> *Hail, self-gendered one,*
> *invisible, fiery begetter of light.*
>
> *Enter into this fire, and fill it.*
> *Let you who dwell within shine through.*

[pause here for a flicker or shift to
indicate that the welcome has been
extended]

> *Open my eyes. Open my eyes.*
> *Great serpent of the East,*
>
> *dawn-riser, great craftsman,*
> *open to me this vessel of flame*
>
> *upon the primeval waters.*
> *Speak to me through this mouth,*

breathe upon me with this light,
and open for me the gate I seek.

VII.   Allow your witch-sight to perceive a
glowing passage into the hot core of the
earth in the bluest part of the flame. When
you are ready, depart your physical body,
and pass through.

A Rite of the Shadow (Via Umbrum)

I.   Arrange your altar. If you do not yet have your own approach to altar work, I recommend a pleasing arrangement of flora (dried flowers, leaves, or branches to represent the Lady or Queen of Elphame) and fauna (bones, teeth, etc., to represent the Devil or King of Elphame) as well as a central candle.

II.   Begin by breathing deeply and relaxing your body. Quiet your bodily senses, and awaken your witch-sight. Consult pp. 53-55 for instructions on this step if needed.

III. If desired, consecrate the space between the worlds using the crossroads charm from p. 66 or the ring of art charm from p. 147.

IV. Call to the Old Ones of your ancestry and your craft in what way seems best to you. If you do not yet have a formula of your own, consider using the one on p. 73.

V.   Meditate upon the forces that
      disempower and enslave you, whatever
      those oppressors may be. When you are
      ready to sever those ties, speak the words:

      Three times do I deny the claim upon my soul.
      I deny the oppressor who would rule me.
      I deny the fear that would restrain me.
      I deny the false friend who would keep me.

VI.   Kneel on one knee, placing one hand
      below your foot and the other on the top
      of your head. Speak the following words,
      feeling yourself freed from those
      previous bonds:

      Eman Hetan, O Eman Hetan,
      From the top of my head
      to the soles of my feet,
      I hold myself within myself.
      Like you, I claim myself for myself,
      and in so doing, become of thee.

VII. When you are ready, feel out with your
      witch-sight the dark figure present in the
      room. Know that what may have
      frightened you before is now your kin,
      your family. It will not harm one of its
      own. Speak freely with the shadow you
      perceive, and when you are ready, ask it

to open for you the hidden door with
these words:

Open for me the Black Book of Art
that I may gaze into its secrets dark.
Obymero per noctem et Symeam
et membres membris
et Lasys cawtis nomis et Arypys.

Bibliography

Agrippa, C. (1533). *Three Books of Occult Philosophy.* R.W. for Gregory Moule.

Allies, J. (1852). *On the Ancient British, Roman, and Saxon Antiquities and Folk-lore of Worcestershire.* United Kingdom: J. H. Parker.

Auricept na nEces. 600-699 CE. Ireland.

Black, G. F. (1894). *Scottish Charms and Amulets.* United Kingdom: Neill and Company.

Buile Shuibi. 1100-1199 CE. Ireland.

Bruno, G. (1582). *Ars Memoriae.*

Bruno, G. (1591). *De Imaginum, Signorum et Idearum Compositione.*

Canon Episcopi. 900 C.E.

Carmichael, A. (1900). *Carmina Gadelica: Hymns and Incantations with Illustrative Notes on Words, Rites, and Customs, Dying and Obsolete: Orally Collected in the Highlands and Islands of Scotland and Translated into English.* Edinburgh.

Cochrane, R. (2016). *The Taper That Lights The Way: Robert Cochrane's Letters*

Revealed. United Kingdom: Mandrake of Oxford.

Colles, A. (1887). A Witches' Ladder. *The Folk-Lore Journal,* 5(1), 1-5.

Dalyell, J. G. (1834). *The Darker Superstitions of Scotland: Illustrated from History and Practice*. United Kingdom: Waugh and Innes.

D'Arcy, P. (2017). What the Mysterious Symbols Made by Early Humans Can Teach Us about How We Evolved. *TED Conferences.* https://ideas.ted.com/what-the-mysterious-symbols-made-by-early-humans-can-teach-us-about-how-we-evolved/

Davis, H. J. (1975). *The Silver Bullet and Other American Witch Stories*. Jonathan David Publishers.

Dioscorides, P. (50 C.E.). *De Materia Medica.*

Du Nay, A. (1977). *The Early History of the Rumanian Language*. United States: Jupiter Press.

Duns, D. D. (1896). On stone folklore. *Journal of the Transactions of the Victoria Institute,* 28. London.

Evans-Wentz, W. Y. (1911). *The Fairy-faith in Celtic Countries*. United Kingdom: H. Frowde.

Frazier, J. G. (1922). *The Golden Bough: A Study in*

Magic and Religion. Macmillan.

Gaselee, S., & Adlington, W. (1915). *The Golden Ass: Being the Metamorphoses of Lucius Apuleius*. United Kingdom: Heinemann.

Guazzo, F. M. (1608). *Compendium Maleficarum*. Apud Haeredes August.

Green, P. B. (1899). *A History of Nursery Rhymes*. United Kingdom: Greening.

Grieve, M. (1971). *A Modern Herbal, Vol. I*. United States: Dover Publications.

Grieve, M. (1971). *A Modern Herbal, Vol. II*. United States: Dover Publications.

Grim, J. A. (1987). *The Shaman: Patterns of Religious Healing Among the Ojibway Indians*. United Kingdom: University of Oklahoma Press.

Guerber, H. A. (1995). *Myths of Northern Lands*. United States: Biblo-Moser.

Hatsis, T. (2015). *The Witches' Ointment: The Secret History of Psychedelic Magic*. United States, Inner Traditions/Bear.

The History of Witches, Ghosts, and Highland Seers: Containing Many Wonderful Well-attested Relations of Supernatural Appearances, Etc. (1800). (n.p.): R. Taylor.

Hopkins, M. (1647). *The Discovery of Witches*. London.

Howard, M. (2013). *Scottish Witches and Warlocks*. United Kingdom: Three Hands Press.

Huson, P. (1971). *The Devil's Picturebook: The Compleat Guide to Tarot Cards: Their Origins and Their Usage*. Putnam.

In Lebor Ogaim. (1300-1399 CE). Ireland.

Jackson, N. (2016). *Fortuna's Wheel: Mysteries of Medieval Tarot*. Renaissance Astrology.

Jakobsen, M. D. (1999). *Shamanism: Traditional and Contemporary Approaches to the Mastery of Spirits and Healing*. United States, Berghahn Books.

Jones, R. (1584). *A Mirrour for Magistrates of Cyties, with Sundrie Grave Orations: and Hereunto is Added a Touchstone for the Time, Containyng Many Perillous Mischiefes, Bred in the Bouels of the Citie of London: By the Infection of Some of Thease Sanctuaries of Iniquitie*.

Kirk, R., & Lang, A. (1893). *The Secret Commonwealth of Elves, Fauns & Fairies: A Study in Folk-lore & Psychical Research* [Original manuscript dated 1691]. United Kingdom, D. Nutt.

Kramer, H. (1487). *The Malleus Maleficarum*. Speyer.

Kuklin, A. (February 1999). *How Do Witches Fly?*. DNA Press.

Leland, C. G. (1891). *Gypsy Sorcery and Fortune-telling: Illustrated by Numerous Incantations, Specimens of Medical Magic, Anecdotes, and Tales*. United States: Dover Publications.

Leland, C. G. (1892). *Etruscan Roman Remains in Popular Tradition*. (n.p.): Fisher Unwin.

Leland, C. G. (1899). *Aradia: Or, The Gospel of the Witches of Italy*. United Kingdom: D. Nutt.

Martin, R. (1989). *Witchcraft and the Inquisition in Venice*. Blackwell Publications.

Mikanowski, J. (2016, March 11). Were the Mysterious Bog People Human Sacrifices? *The Atlantic*. https://www.theatlantic.com/science/archive/2016/03/were-europes-mysterious-bog-people-human-sacrifices/472839/

Murray, A. (1921). *The Witch-Cult in Western Europe*. Oxford, Clarendon Press.

Murray, A. (1931). *The God of the Witches*. Sampson, Low, Marston, and Co.

Nash, D. W. (1858). *Taliesin, Or, The Bards and Druids of Britain: A Translation of the Remains of the Earliest Welsh Bards, and an Examination of the Bardic Mysteries*. United

Kingdom: J.R. Smith.

Oehlanschlaeger, A. (1821). Hagbarth and Signa; A Tragedy. *Blackwood's Edinburgh Magazine.* Edinburgh.

Parpola, S. (1993). The Assyrian Tree of Life: Tracing the Origins of Jewish Monotheism and Greek Philosophy. *Journal of Near Eastern Studies,* 52(3).

Peterson, J. H. (trans.). (2007). *Grimorium Verum.* CreateSpace.

Physiologus. 200 C.E.

The Poetic Edda: Mythological poems. (1969). United Kingdom: Clarendon Press.

Posch, S. (2016). *Was 'Eko Eko Azarak' Originally an Arabic Chant to the Devil?* https://witchesandpagans.com/pagan-culture-blogs/paganistan/was-eko-eko-azarak-originally-an-arabic-chant-to-the-devil.html

Rätsch, C. (2005). *The Encyclopedia of Psychoactive Plants: Ethnopharmacology and Its Applications.* United States, Inner Traditions/Bear.

Risley, H. H. (1903). *Census of India, 1901: Volume I. India. Ethnographic Appendices, Being the Data Upon which the Caste Chapter of the Report is*

Based. India: Office of the Superintendent of Government printing, India.

Roud, S., & Simpson, J. (2000). *A dictionary of English folklore*. United Kingdom: Oxford University Press.

Scot, R. (1584). *The Discoverie of Witchcraft*.

Scott, W. (1830). *Letters on Demonology and Witchcraft, Addressed to J.G. Lockhart, Esq*. United Kingdom: John Murray.

Seymour, S. J. D. (1913). *Irish Witchcraft and Demonology*. Ireland: Norman, Remington.

Stuart, J. C. (1597). *Daemonologie*. Edinburgh.

Timbs, J. (1873). *Doctors and Patients: Or, Anecdotes of the Medical World and Curiosities of Medicine*. United Kingdom: R. Bentley and son.

von Worms, A. (2015). *The Book of Abramelin: A New Translation*. Israel, IBIS Press.

Walker, E. (2008). *Horse*. United Kingdom: Reaktion Books.

Whitehouse, D. (2016). *The Moon: A Biography*. United Kingdom: Orion.

Wilby, E. (2005). *Cunning-folk and familiar spirits : shamanistic visionary traditions in early modern British witchcraft and magic*. United Kingdom: Sussex Academic Press.

Wilby, E. (2010). *The Visions of Isobel Gowdie: Magic, Witchcraft and Dark Shamanism in Seventeenth-century Scotland*. United Kingdom, Sussex Academic Press.

Wright, T. (1843). *A Contemporary Narrative of the Proceedings Against Dame Alice Kyteler, Prosecuted for Sorcery in 1324, by Richard de Ledrede, Bishop of Ossory*. London: The Camden Society.

Roger J. Horne is a writer, folk witch, and modern animist. He is also the author of the *Folk Witchcraft* series. His personal spiritual practice is informed by the magical currents of Scottish cunning craft and Appalachian herb-doctoring. Through his writing, Horne seeks to help other witches rediscover the living tradition of folk craft and connect to their own sacred initiatory threads of lore, land, and familiar spirit. Learn more about him at rogerjhorne.com.

Also by Roger J. Horne:

Folk Witchcraft: A Guide to Lore, Land, and the Familiar Spirit for the Solitary Practitioner

Cartomancy in Folk Witchcraft: Divination, Magic, and Lore

The Witch's Art of Incantation: Spoken Charms, Spells, and Curses in Folk Witchcraft